Sarah and the Garden

Sarah and the Garden

And the Time God Heard Her Laughing

TRICIA HAYES

WIPF *&* STOCK · Eugene, Oregon

SARAH AND THE GARDEN
And the Time God Heard Her Laughing

Wipf & Stock
An Imprint of Wipf and Stock Publishers
199 W. 8th Ave., Suite 3
Eugene, OR 97401

www.wipfandstock.com

PAPERBACK ISBN: 979-8-3852-4021-0
HARDCOVER ISBN: 979-8-3852-4022-7
EBOOK ISBN: 979-8-3852-4023-4

04/17/25

For Sarah

Contents

Preface

THE TENT IS STILL and dim. The heat of the day has thickened around busy hands and has slowed them. Sarah is alone inside the soft, billowing folds of the tent. Silent. Silence. There are no little boys to chase or little girls to teach, so Sarah is quiet in the still heat of the day. When the voices of men break the silence and when the call to hurry cracks the stillness, Sarah whirls into movement—deft, quick, ready action until the work is completed and the tent is still again. Silent. Silence. The folds envelop Sarah and what is within is hidden. "Where is your wife, Sarah?" they ask. Is Sarah already listening at the door of the tent, or does the sound of this name draw her there?

There are stories we tell each other over and over. We know them well, and our children know them well. The best stories have an element of surprise that endures no matter how often we hear them. This is because the surprise is so rich that each time we tell the story we are somehow surprised again. It is as if we can hold the story in our hands like we can hold a prism. It is as if we can slowly turn the story around and around again and each time see light and angle and color that makes us wonder whether we have seen such a thing before, or whether maybe what we are seeing is a brand-new discovery.

Why did Sarah laugh? Is there even an answer to this question? What is the light and angle and color in this story that allows God to ask the question and for such a question to go unanswered? God knows that Sarah has laughed, even though her laughter is hidden "within herself," and God knows that "the way of woman had ceased with Sarah," even though that fact is hidden deep within Sarah also. Why then does God ask why Sarah laughed? Doesn't God already know? Who is the question for?

The story of Sarah in the book of Genesis is not a simple story. There is light and angle and color to see if we just hold it a little longer, if we just turn and ponder and look with fresh eyes. We can ask questions, too. And if we look carefully enough, we may find old things long hidden.

Introduction

It is said that Sarah laughed at God. Imagine laughing at God. It is also said that she laughed because she didn't believe on that day long ago when God came to her tent to tell her she would have a son. But sometimes things are said out of a particular kind of darkness that is the result of closed eyes, and when we open our eyes to look at things more carefully, we find there is more to the story than we thought. Sarah's laughter happens inside Sarah's story. So, her laughter must be understood inside that story, not isolated to the moment in Genesis 18 when Sarah laughs.

When we read any story in the Bible, we must think about how we are reading it. So, in the first chapter of part one we will briefly discuss how we read the Bible. The study of how we read the Bible is a fascinating one, and I have spent happy hours engaged in it. I would like to share some things I have learned for myself with you. My hope is that they will hone your approach to the text as they have honed mine, and perhaps even increase your joy as you read. For though my primary purpose is to illuminate Sarah, I also hope the time you spend in this book will help you think about how you interact with the Bible.

Now Sarah's story begins all the way back in the garden, that beautiful old garden where God created unity, and where humanity broke it. The entire narrative of the Bible emerges out of this broken unity, what happens to people because of it, and what God is doing to fix it. We will think about these things as we think about Sarah, because Sarah's laughter itself has to do with the garden. It has to do with unity broken, what happens to people because of it, and what God is doing to fix it.

Therefore, the second chapter of part one is about the garden. We will study the garden to see what God's intention for humanity and for the world was before unity broke. We will look at who the man and the woman were before and after the matter of the tree. Understanding how God intended things to be and considering what they have become will help us with Sarah.

In the third chapter of part one, we will introduce two terms that illustrate the broken unity that happened in the garden. They are terms I came up with after noticing that the priorities of the men and of the women of Genesis correspond to the words of the curse.

For the men the curse has to do with the ground. For the women, it has to do with the seed. The men are concerned with things having to do with the land of Israel, walking it, digging wells, its fertility. The women are concerned with the seed of Israel, producing and protecting children. I began to think of men as Landholders and women as Linekeepers. These terms are not exhaustive. However, they are a way to think about the practical impact of what happened to humanity after the tree, how what was meant for humanity to do together becomes separated.

This division of labor between the Linekeepers and the Landholders will inform the rest of our study. There are three themes that arise from this division. First, we will think about how God created the woman from a central, protective place in humanity and how, even after the curse, her actions remind us of this. Second, we will think about how though human beings were created to be "help like the help of God" for each other, that help is compromised after the tree. We will see how God supplies help to humanity where humanity ought to have been help for each other. Third, though the cursed state of humanity is not God's intention, God lets the curse stand. God does not change events in order to thwart even the most awful effects of the curse. This is confusing and maddening. But strangely, even though God allows the curse to stand, there are times in the story when God contradicts and works against it.

We see this pattern beginning with Eve and continuing with Sarah and the Linekeepers after her. The women immediately suffer the effects of the curse. The men are firmly at the forefront of the action seemingly happy to have the women hidden in the background. However, though God does not reprimand or force change in the men, God interacts with the women in ways that work towards fixing things.

In part two, we will focus on three pericopes within Sarah's story. Each emerge out of the destruction of unity that happened in the garden. Together they help to explain her laughter and to point to what God is doing to fix things.

The first pericope is in Genesis 12 when Abraham asks Sarah to say she is his sister as they enter Egypt. He asks her to do this so that "it may go well with me because of you, and that I may live on account of you." We will discuss how this pericope initiates Sarah as a Linekeeper. She is the first protector of Israel. We will discuss how the Joseph narrative in Genesis works to illuminate and magnify Sarah as a protector. When Sarah's story is echoed in Joseph's, it becomes clear that Sarah is more than just help for Abraham; she is an effective blessing to the entire world. It really does go well because of her.

The second pericope is in Genesis 18 when Sarah laughs and asks a question. Sarah's question is as ponderous as the one God asks the woman in the garden. It loops Sarah's story back to Eden and propels it forward into the rest of the story of Scripture. This moment at Sarah's tent shows us that Yahweh is a God who hears and sees hidden things.

The third pericope is in Genesis 21. After Isaac is born, Sarah exclaims, "God has made laughter for me; everyone who hears will laugh with me." This second bout of laugher prophecies the great nation that will come from Sarah's seed. We will explore the question: Who might be laughing with Sarah? by looking at the significance of Hagar and Ishmael. Sarah's laughter sings what God began in the shadow of the garden and in the hiddenness of Sarah's tent. Her laughter remembers what God did for her, and what God will continue to do for anyone who might laugh along with Sarah.

My hope for our study of Sarah is that it will give us fresh eyes to see and tuned ears to hear. Perhaps when we look up from our Bibles and put aside this book, we might each of us on our own think about Sarah's laughter and what it means to be beloved of the God who sees and hears. For I am not interested in telling you how to ponder Sarah's laughter for yourself. I only desire to guide you, through careful study, to pull Sarah out of her hidden place. Once we have done that, however you laugh with Sarah is yours to laugh.

PART ONE

CHAPTER 1

How We Read the Bible and Some Things to Consider Before We Begin

THE BIBLE IS AN interaction of many voices. It is not a record of one voice, as if its words were dictated to a human author from some distant place in the sky.

The Bible is an interaction of many voices. The voices of narrators, the voices of biblical characters, voices even beyond the scope of the Bible that spoke across generations into the lives of the human authors, voices that speak into the life experience of readers today. The varied voices act like a prism that can be turned to play light and angle and color, and the Bible breathes the breath of God.

Good exegesis is the humble effort to hear the voices. There are more technical definitions of exegesis, but really when it comes down to it, a good search of the depths of the word of God begins with the effort to hear. God speaks to us through the words printed on the pages of the Bible, but God also speaks through what is not said, through twists and gaps in the text that invite us to stop, think, and question.

Sometimes through these twists and gaps we catch a shot of light that might just let us in on a deeper hearing, a deeper seeing. Sometimes we hear the almighty voice that acknowledges pain and joy not only in the lives of the biblical characters but also in the lives of we ourselves who read.

Reading the Bible in this way—by yielding humbly to the varied voices—is unbound by the constraints of past interpretation. There is always something new to see. However, this does not mean we operate without careful boundaries.

When we say "good exegesis is the humble effort to hear the voices," what do we mean? The word "exegesis" comes from the Greek word meaning to "lead out." Exegesis is the careful study to lead out or to interpret the text's meaning. We study Greek and Hebrew to understand why the authors choose certain words and why they are put together the way they are. We study history and archaeology, literary genre, geography, and weather to hone our understanding to what the author may have intended to convey. We also study how an individual story fits within its section, its biblical book, its testament, and finally the entire story of the Bible. These are some of the tools of exegesis—things that help us get at what might have been the original intention of the human author, and in doing so, help us get at what God might intend for us to gain from his word.

Perhaps one of the best ways to understand exegesis is to think about its opposite. If exegesis is pulling meaning out of the text, eisegesis is putting meaning into the text. We commit eisegesis when we inject a meaning that suits our own theology or purposes. We commit eisegesis when we try to see in the text what we want to see, or what we think the text ought to be saying instead of wrestling with what is there. Exegesis is harder than eisegesis. Eisegesis finds answers we already thought we knew, as if we went ahead of ourselves and planted them there to find without looking. Exegesis asks good questions, questions that have us looking deep into the surrounding story for answers, questions that might just lead to more questions.

Good exegesis involves humble effort. We love to think of the Bible as God's special word to each one of us, and it is right to feel intimately connected to God and to seek the message he has for us. However, we must remember that the Bible was not originally written to you and me. To say that the Bible is an interaction of varied voices is to say, among other things, that it is unique to anything else that has ever been written and that it has the power to speak through those voices. However, this is not to say that the Bible can mean anything and everything. To say "this is what this passage means to me" without regard for the careful study of what the author may have intended is risky. The author intended the words on the page to mean something, and though the Bible speaks in many ways to all different people in all different times, we must subject our understanding to the careful standards of exegesis. Humble study prevents the dead ends and unsound theology that can only confuse us and others.

The ideas we will explore in this study are unconstrained by traditional interpretations that have ruled the day for centuries. Our study may yield conclusions that are new, for we are looking at the story with fresh eyes. For instance, Sarah's laughter in Gen 18 has been interpreted over and over again as a sign of her lack of faith, and her casting out of Hagar as the petulance of a woman who failed to be an advocate for another woman. God's assertion that Sarah did indeed laugh is traditionally interpreted to assume that God is catching Sarah in a lie. A closer read and some humble listening just might yield something else. We will study Sarah's story using five guidelines.

EVERYTHING GOES BACK TO THE GARDEN

Our first guideline is to recognize that Sarah's story begins in the garden. We will consider Eve when we consider Sarah. We will think about the relationship of the man and the woman in the garden before and after the curse when we interpret what is going on with Abraham and Sarah. The curse meant something for all humanity, but it also meant something different for the man than it did for the woman. Thinking about this and trying to get a handle on those differences will help us to understand Sarah.

One of my rules of exegesis is that I try to recognize this type of thing everywhere in the Bible. Really, the garden informs the entire story of the Bible, and the entire story of the Bible informs each individual story within it. So, when we look at Sarah (or anyone for that matter), we must look at her story in the light of the rest of the Sarah narrative in Genesis, the book of Genesis, the Torah, the Hebrew Scriptures, and then finally the New Testament. Simply put, we will fail to understand biblical narrative unless we seek first to understand each story within the greater story.

THERE IS A DIFFERENCE BETWEEN INTERPRETATION AND TEXT

Our second guideline is to recognize that there are some interpretations of the Bible that have become so culturally accepted that they are widely mistaken for the text itself. Careful exegesis requires that we distinguish between what the text says and what people say it says. For instance, if we go back to the garden and re-read the narrative, we find that it does not say the fruit the woman offered the man was an apple, and it does not say the woman enticed the man with her sexual wiles. However, if we look at how that story has been interpreted in both writing and art, we find apples and sex everywhere.

If the text does not tell us how a character felt, or their motives for doing something, we simply cannot assume we know. We can look carefully at the rest of the story and look for clues in its context, and we can listen for what is said and ponder what is unsaid. But if the story does not tell us how someone felt or why they did what they did, there is a reason for the silence. There is something to be pondered in the silence. The lack of explanation does not mean that the author missed something or made a mistake.

Traditional interpretation has tended to fill silences with explanations. Instead, we will ponder the silences. In many cases, it is better to ask good questions of the text than to seek immovable answers. After all, the Bible is above all God's word. If we quickly fill in the gaps with our own explanations, wipe our hands, and consider our understanding complete, we miss deep and unsearchable things.[1]

You will find my own imaginative reflections in italicized entries throughout the book. This is, I think, something the gaps and silences in the story invite us to do. We can indeed play with the text in this way.[2] These are distinguished in italics because though they arise out of my careful study, they are not scholarly conclusions. They are artistic reflections. If the text does not tell us how a character felt, we cannot know, but we can consider ideas and imagine. However, we must not pin the text down to these things as if our own musing determines meaning.

MANY FACETS

The third guideline is closely related to the second. God's word is meditation literature. Each story is meticulously written and complex. The more we turn it, the more it will gift us with light and angle and color. We will see new things as we study Sarah. But we will not see all the things. We will not view her story in the single way it is meant to be viewed because that single way does not exist.

THE WORDS LIVE ON THE PAGE

Our fourth guideline has to do with what the Bible *does*. The Bible infuses meaning into the story of God's interaction with humanity. Often the meaning of the story flies higher than the experience of the character. Words and actions might bear greater significance to the reader than they do to the character. Meaning is often

---

1 Sharp indicates, "Silence can indicate a focus elsewhere, or it can compel the reader's attention with all the power of an urgent whisper in a crowded room. It is a challenge and a joy for the interpreter to learn, over years of study and reflection, how to listen well to silences in literature." Sharp, *Wresting with the Word*, 28.

2. Brueggemann quotes Raymond Brown: "After all, in the Scriptures we are in our Father's house where the children are permitted to play." Brueggemann, *Introduction to the Old Testament*, xiii.

informed by more than the moment in which the story is set, for we understand meaning with the entire story of Scripture in mind. This of course goes beyond the scope of understanding of any one character who lives in any one time and place.

But the words live on the page and mean living things. An individual character may or may not understand the greater significance of what they have said or done, but the human author might, and the divine author certainly does. With the help of the rest of the story of Scripture, the reader might, too.[3]

GOD'S VOICE OF LOVE

Fifth, there is something particular about the Bible that distinguishes it from anything else that has ever been written. Though it is a work of many human voices over time and different places, it is the voice of Yahweh. This is the voice that comes from the love of the God who intended good for creation and who saw humanity corrupt it at the cost of its own broken heart. It is the voice of the God who is determined to see his good intention through despite human corruption. It is the voice of the God who hears the cries of humanity.

But, especially for our understanding of Sarah, we must consider that the voice who speaks to the great patriarchs and kings, judges, and prophets is the same one who speaks to the hidden, the hurt, the cast aside. This voice comes from the one whose "loving-kindness is everlasting, who remembers us in our low estate" (Ps 136:23).

The humans whose oral and written tradition constitute the Bible were humans who spent much of their history in "low estate."[4] There were rare times when the Jews enjoyed sovereignty

---

3. Brown indicates, "The sensus plenior is that additional, deeper meaning, intended by God but not clearly intended by the human author, which is seen to exist in the words of a biblical text (or group of texts, or even a whole book) when they are studied in the light of further revelation or development in the understanding of revelation." Brown, *Sensus Plenior of Sacred Scripture*, 92.

4. Brueggemann, *Introduction to the Old Testament*, 23.

and security, but most often they were subject to the powerful succession of ancient empires who ruled with harsh hands. The literature that comes from this people reflects this experience.

Though most of the Bible was penned by men, the memory and oral tradition that informed it surely reflects the heart and experience of the women who spoke God's stories to their little ones. These two things—the political situation of the Jewish people and the influence of the voice of women—are keys to understanding even the texts that sing glory and prosperity for Israel. When we consider Israel's history, we might consider that Scripture's depiction of its women under the yoke of patriarchy, and the injustice that came of that yoke, reflects Israel's own experience. Israel was rarely and only in short spurts the glorious victor. She was most often oppressed and ruled over. Israel herself might relate more closely to the woman under the yoke of patriarchy than with the man who wields it.

The Bible arises out of a world burdened by patriarchy. The events of the story and the worldview of the human authors reflect patriarchy. But that does not mean God's heart accepts patriarchy.

Remember, there is a difference between the text and the interpretation of the text. It is essential to our understanding of who God is and who we are as humans to see that God is not complicit in the horrible things we do to each other. The people who wrote the Bible, and the people who read and interpret the Bible, live in the mess humanity has made of this world. As we said above, the Bible was not dictated or dropped down from heaven. It has human fingerprints all over it and every single one of them reflects the curse.

There are things in the Bible that are horribly disturbing, but that does not mean God agrees with them. It means that human minds and hearts are intertwined in the writing of what is also God's word. This can be confusing and maddening when we interact with stories in which God seems to be standing by blithely allowing awful things to happen.

There are many interpreters who feel that these horrible things in the Bible (often done by the so-called heroes of our faith, like Abraham selling Sarah into Pharaoh's harem so that he himself is safe) render the Bible so patriarchal as to be irredeemable. I do not agree with this. I see a deep current that runs within the narrative that subverts what is at first read infuriating and alienating. If we only read the text on its most basic level and fail to see beyond the human fingerprints, we will remain infuriated and alienated.

If we read the horrible with the entire story in mind, we find that the love of God is the deep running current. We see God's action against the horrible and his heart of love towards each one of us. This pattern is one of the reasons Sarah's story is so fascinating. The way God interacts with Sarah is a microcosm of God's loving interaction with the hidden and brokenhearted.

A fellow seminary student angrily told me that my sort of thinking is only just giving the Bible a bye because it is the Bible. I do not think so. I think the heart of God is hidden in the background with the brokenhearted. It is behind the clamor of what is at the forefront of the narrative. If we do not see this, it is not because it is not there.

The voices of low estate are like the subtle background color of a mosaic we must fix our eyes steadily to see, or like a leitmotif that plays softly in the background of an opera. Though they reside in the background, almost hidden, they are the structure of the piece. To mistake them is to miss the piece. So, we listen still and silent for the voice of the one who sees and hears, and who affirms the people in their pain.

One of the finest examples of the hearing, seeing, and affirming voice of Yahweh in the Scriptures is the moment Sarah laughs, and Yahweh responds.

CHAPTER 2

Everything Really Does
Go Back to the Garden

To UNDERSTAND THE MOTHER of nations, we go back to the mother
of the living, because Sarah's story begins in the beginning. Sarah's
story is about the destruction that came after the matter of the tree,
what we call the curse. But it does not begin there. It begins in the
garden with what God intended for her and for her children.

When we meet Sarah, she is far from Eden. Her life is a picture of broken unity. That is why we go back to the garden before
we peer into Sarah's tent, because the garden is about unity created,
unity broken, and God's promise of unity restored.

When we study anything in the Bible, we go back to the garden to remember what God intended so that we are not fooled
into thinking the pain we see is how things are supposed to be
or will always be, or worst of all, that the current state of things is
okay with God. Studying what God intended for humanity helps
us to see God's loving action even in the midst of the chaotic effects of the curse that might hide it if we are not paying attention.
Somehow in understanding the gash humanity's disobedience
struck across the face of creation the mysterious things of what
God means for us and for the earth become clearer. We see the
shadow of the intention in the reality of the destruction.

GOD'S INTENTION IS UNITY

The unity God created was a deep unity. It was an everything unity. In the beginning, the realm of God and the realm of humans were united in a high garden place where rivers ran down and they all walked together. When God created the woman, he created unity right from the start and formed her from the center of the man. She is distinct from the man, yet she is made from him. In Eden, the man and the woman had the kind of unity heaven and earth had. Different but unified.

Therefore, as we begin our study, we must stop calling the mother of the living "Eve." We really should not call her "the mother of the living" yet either. In the beginning, before the effects of the curse, the two people in the garden are called "humanity." They are the man and the woman. The reason we call the man Adam is because that name sounds like the Hebrew word for humanity. The reason we call the woman Eve is because the man names her this when they leave Eden. But before the curse, the man and the woman are humanity, man and woman, not Adam and Eve.

This is an important distinction. If we are going to have any shot at applying God's intention for humanity to the story of Sarah, we must try to see the beginning of the story for what it is, not for what it becomes. This is quite challenging with the Bible, but I do not think it is impossible. We do this all the time when we are reading other stories. We read them in order. We know that if we impose later developments of the story upon things that happened before, we will fail to experience the story the way the author intends for us to experience it. We would no more have Cinderella's coach turn back into a pumpkin before she attends the ball than we should read "cursed" into the part of the biblical narrative that is not yet cursed.

Even so, the challenge with the Bible that distinguishes it from anything else we read is that it reveals the truest of truths. It is no fairy tale. It is humanity's story and God's story. Because we are deeply entrenched in it, it is hard to peer at it from a place we are not.

"Eve" is different than "the woman." So is Sarah, and so are we. We live in a world that suffers the aftermath of the curse. Our perception of reality, how we read, relate, and understand is affected by the curse. Though it is natural for us to look at the story through a post-curse lens, we must try to break free from that and read the story with fresh eyes. What was it like in the beginning, when things were just what God intended them to be? There is a difference between who the man and the woman are before and after the tree, and if we mix them up, we will compromise our understanding of the story.

Genesis 1:26–28 can help us with this. It is the guiding statement for our understanding of the garden narrative. It tells us what God intended for creation. Anything that happens before the tree can be interpreted considering God's stated intention in Gen 1:26–28, and anything after, its perversion.

> Then God said, "Let us make humanity in our image, according to our likeness; and let them rule over the fish of the sea and over the birds of the sky and over the cattle and over all the earth, and over every creeping thing that creeps on the earth." God created humanity in his own image, in the image of God he created him, male and female he created them. God blessed them; and God said to them, "Be fruitful and multiply, and fill the earth, and subdue it; and rule over the fish of the sea and over the birds of the sky and over every living thing that moves on the earth. (Gen 1:26–28)

What can we learn about what God intended for humanity and the earth by reading Gen 1:26–28?

UNITY CREATES UNITY

First, we see that right from the start in Gen 1:26, unity created unity. Whatever the mysterious "let us" statement means, at the very least we know that there was some sort of fellowship going on when the world was created. Therefore, a key to understanding the little poem that follows in Gen 1:27 is to see that God's image has to do with some sort of fellowship too.

Some interpret "let us" to mean that Jesus was the worker of the Father's creation. Others propose that God was interacting with the heavenly council of beings we see periodically throughout the Bible. For us, at this point in our study, we resist trying to define and limit this mystery, not because we do not believe whatever we believe about how God created the universe, but because at the moment of Gen 1:26, the word of God does not tell us. It simply says, "Let us." When it comes down to it, we do not know exactly what "let us" means, except that there was an "us" at the creation of humanity, and that this "us" is essential to what it means to be made in God's image. Unity created unity.

Sometimes we talk about God as an entity who transcends gender. We think our personal pronouns for God are only stabs at comprehending an identity beyond our comprehension. When we use masculine or feminine images for God it is because we think it is in humanizing God that we can begin to understand God. However, this is backwards. We do not understand God as male and female like humanity. We understand humanity as male and female like God. We understand who we are by meditating on who God is. God is somehow a perfect unity of maleness and femaleness. God intended for humanity to be like God, a unity of male and female.

Mother Eagle. Father God. Open tent and carrying arms.[1] His peace, his breast, his lap, his comfort, our Mother.[2] Heart raging womb[3] bearing compassion moving arms aching Mother Father God. Open tent,[4] sheltering wings.[5]God's heart rages like a mother bear.[6] We are born of God.[7]

---

1. Isa 46:3–4.

2. Isa 66:12–13.

3. Exod 34:6. The Hebrew word for "compassion" is in the same semantic range as the word for "womb."

4. Ps 61:4. Also tent/woman imagery in the OT.

5. Ps 91:4.

6. Hos 13:8.

7. Deut 32:18.

UNITY IS ESSENTIAL

The second thing Gen 1:26–28 can show us is that God commands humanity to be fruitful and multiply, fill, subdue, and rule the earth *before the matter of the tree*. To obey the command in the way that images God, male and female must work together. Once unity is broken at the tree, humanity will continue to fill and rule the earth, but they will do it in a way that reflects and multiplies the curse. Once the unity of male and female is destroyed at the tree, human rule becomes a perversion of God's intention.

WHAT IS RULE ANYWAY?

God commands humanity to fill, rule, and subdue the earth. The words "rule" and "subdue" are strong words in English and in Hebrew. Neither word sounds like something that would reflect the gracious governance of God. They sound too harsh, and indeed, in our post-curse world we associate ruling and subduing with harsh things like power and hierarchy.

We look up from our Bibles and try to imagine ruling and subduing without hierarchy. We hardly can. For us, on this side of the curse, ruling and subduing seem to go together naturally with hierarchy. However, if human rule is bound by the guiding statement that it is a gift given to humanity as God's image, human rule has nothing to do with hierarchy.

Our ideas of ruling and subduing are more influenced by their corruption than their intention, so we think of them as negative or harsh. However, when we consider God's intention, and not the corruption we sit in, we ponder what it would have looked like if humanity had used this great power well, within God's established bounds.

Anyone who lives on this earth can agree that it is a dangerous and unpredictable place. What if the earth needed to be subdued, and the only way to subdue it properly was for humanity to work in perfect unity with each other to make it into something much more friendly and hospitable than it is today? What if the earth was meant to be subdued by the multiplication of God's image so much that the earth would work for us and with us? Not only would the ground yield good crops, but the oceans would not sweep away homes and lions would not attack people. What if humanity would not have broken that one fleshed union at the tree? What if the maleness and femaleness given to humanity, used in unity, would have enabled humanity to subject the earth to such goodness that the whole place would have become a garden for us?

Without unity, humanity is unable to wrestle the earth into a hospitable home. Without unity, the strong hand of unified rule becomes the harsh hand that mistreats the earth and its inhabitants. The earth is no garden. It is as dangerous and unpredictable as the humans who rule it.

Humanity must reflect unity seamlessly. Unless the maleness and femaleness given to both are used together by each, humanity cannot do what God made us to do. What happened in the garden tore apart the foundation of what it means to be human and how humanity is meant to be on this earth.

Unfortunately, much traditional interpretation and common discussion of the garden does not distinguish who the man and the woman are pre-tree and post-tree, so our understanding of who they were intended to be, and who they have become, can be muddied and swirled together.

The man and the woman of the garden are uniformly called "Adam and Eve," regardless of whether the discussion has to do with the time before or after the curse. But it is important to note that the names "Adam" and "Eve" are names that reflect the division that came after the matter of the tree. The man and the woman are ontologically different before the tree and after. Because this change is so fundamental we must distinguish it when we discuss "the man and the woman" or "Adam and Eve."

Our discussion will attempt to clean up our understanding. First, we will clear away some common assumptions about the garden that have come from traditional interpretation. After we have done that, we will be free to observe some unique characteristics of how the woman was created and how the man was created. We will see how even though they are particular to the male or the female at their inception in the garden, they were meant to be used together.

TRADITIONAL INTERPRETATION AND THE WORD OF THE BIBLE

We are on solid ground to say that there are two garden stories, the one written in the Bible, and the one people have created over millennia of interpretation. Traditional interpretation and Renaissance art have imagined the woman in the garden as a tempting seductress who lures the innocent man into eating an apple. He is the authentic image of God, since he was created first. After all, both he and God are males, so that's that. The woman was created second, to be a helper. The man needed someone to serve him and take care of him, and God did not want the man to do without, so God created a woman—a helpful sidekick.

Unfortunately, the woman is connected to sin, in cahoots with the snake, who is, of course, Satan.[8] She is foolish at best to listen to the snake, and she is evil at worst to draw the man into the snare of seeking wisdom apart from God. If it were not for the woman's sin, things would be a whole lot better in the world. We might even still be in the wonderful garden. This is the reason that the beauty and sexuality of women is something to be suspicious of. If it led the first man down the wrong path, it will lead all men down the wrong path. So, although her beauty and sexuality are part of who she is, and although its depiction makes for some gorgeous art, that part must be suppressed. A woman's sexuality is connected to the original sin of humankind. It is right there in the Bible. Before the woman messed up, humanity was naked and unashamed. After she messed up, they were naked and something else that caused all sorts of problems between men and women. Whatever that "something else" is, it has to do with sex. So, in a

---

8. Later interpretation and Second Temple literature has connected the serpent with Satan. In Genesis however, the entity in the garden is not identified as Satan—he is a serpent.

very real sense, the woman in the garden asked for the trouble and the sexual violence that resulted from her sin. Clearly women need to be placed in a subordinate position to men. Look at the trouble they cause! You can see it all the way back to the garden. It is right and even biblical for men to have a position of primacy over women.

Or, thinking a different way, maybe the serpent waited for the woman to be created to bother to engage in conversation. She is a much more intelligent discussion partner. The man is a follower. All it took for the man to eat the fruit was for the woman to hand it to him. No consideration, no conversation, no reflection. The man simply ate.[9] This probably had to do with sex, too.

What did Adam do? What did Eve think? Who is guilty of what? Can what happened in the garden show us that women really are the brains of the operation? Or maybe the garden shows us that women are trouble-making tempters who deserve punishment. Or perhaps the serpent waited to approach the woman because women are easily beguiled fools. In that case maybe the garden narrative really does justify men's rule over women, unless of course the garden proves that men are aimless dolts ready to be led around by their stomachs and their sex drives.

Does this all this sound familiar? We could go on and on, and many have. However, the problem is that all these ideas, and others like them, are founded on one simple error; they impose the effects of the curse on the story before the story itself does. When we open our Bibles, and look at what is written there, we see something quite different from how it has so often been interpreted. The fruit is not an apple, and the woman is no sidekick. There is nothing about the woman using her sexual wiles to entice the man to take the fruit. She simply gives it to him, and he eats.

There are many reasons why the discrepancy between what the Bible says and how it has traditionally been interpreted is a problem. When we replace what God says in the Bible with what people have said about it, and then give it the primacy and weight we give God's word, we are not simply short-circuiting our chance

9. Trible, *God and the Rhetoric of Sexuality*, 113.

of understanding; we do actual damage. The misinterpretation of the garden story has been used to justify the mistreatment of women,[10] which causes us to misunderstand God. When Scripture is misused like this, it is not a far jump to assume that God thinks it is okay to treat woman differently than men.

For our purposes the issue of importance here is to see that the misinterpretation of the garden leads us astray from the main point of the garden. And when we miss the main point of the garden, we miss the main point of the whole story, and the questions we ask of the text become skewed.

A careful look at the garden reveals that it is interpretation, not the narrative itself, that has led us to think that it is about sex. Once we determine that the garden is more about unity created and unity broken than it is about Eve being a tempting seductress, we can begin to ask better questions because we are not limiting our questions of the garden to what the garden is only barely about. Instead, we broaden them to what it is mainly about. What happened in the garden was a cataclysmic break that affected every inch of the universe and every person who would ever be born into it. This cataclysm is our starting point and plumb line for the questions we ask about the garden, and therefore the questions we ask about Sarah.

God's work that arises out of the disaster of the garden involves fixing broken unity—our relationships with each other, with the earth, and with God. If the garden is only about what happened between a husband and wife, God's work through all time would be limited to redeeming heterosexual relationships. But what happened in the garden is broader than interpretation's limits, for what happened in the garden was fundamental to all relationships everywhere, and that is what God is fixing—all relationships everywhere.

---

10. Jimmy Carter, in a 2015 TED talk entitled, "Why I Believe the Mistreatment of Women Is The Number One Human Rights Abuse," said that it is a misinterpretation of Scripture that "relegates women to a secondary position to men in the eyes of God."

We ask questions of what we are reading with anything we read, and the Bible is no exception. If our questions arise from an interpretation of the text that is not grounded in the text itself, we will miss the illuminating insights it is offering to us. For instance, when we read the garden narrative, we find that the man and the woman are naked. We wonder if their nakedness has to do with sex. We wonder this because we are accustomed to the depiction of nakedness in the garden as having to do with sex.

But what if we break free and look carefully at the text? How is the word "naked" working in the context of the story? There are other things associated with nakedness after all. Perhaps nakedness has to do with birth or infancy? Or perhaps it has to do with being like the animals? These are good questions, and when we begin to research the word, we find that some answers stand a greater chance of getting at the point than others do. Some answers are carefully grounded in the language of the text. Others rely on assumptions.

Once the assumption that nakedness has to do with sex is in place, everything else in the garden gets linked to sex too. If the garden is about sex, surely the woman was able to get the man to eat the fruit by tempting him with her beautiful naked body. And if Eve is a tempting seductress, it only follows that Sarah, the very next developed female character in the story, must be trouble too. But what if the actions of Sarah and the other women in the Bible are more complex than this?

What if the garden is not all about sex?

THREE NEW QUESTIONS

Let's ask three new questions of the text. First, does "naked and unashamed" really have to do with sex and marriage? Next, does it really matter that the man was created first? Or perhaps the better question is, does it mean what we traditionally think it means that the man was created first? Finally, is "helper" the best way to understand who the woman was created to be?

NAKED AND UNASHAMED

Let's have a closer look at the phrase "naked and unashamed." With any question we ask of the text, we begin by looking at where it sits on the page. What is its context? What are the ideas and images that surround the simply stated fact that humanity was "naked and unashamed?"

In Gen 2:23, God completes humanity by creating the woman. Let us stop here and think about that. We are accustomed to thinking of this as the moment God creates a woman to be a marriage partner to the man. But the text does not say this. It says that God created a "woman" (*ishah*) because it is not good for humanity to be alone. The Hebrew word for "woman" (*ishah*) runs throughout the entire narrative of Gen 2–3.

Ishah is translated "wife" in Gen 2:24–25 when the text is talking about the man leaving his father and mother and clinging to his wife. But the word is still *ishah*. It does not change to something different to signify "wife." There are other Hebrew words for wife, but the writer chose *ishah*, "woman." This means that the choice of the translator can make the text about marriage and a wife, or about humanity and a woman.

What if we translated the *ishah* of Gen 2:24–25 as "woman" instead of "wife"? When we do this, the verses become more about unity in diversity. They are not limited to marriage. This is not to say that the text cannot honor and inform marriage. But since the writer does not use a word specific to wife, we must consider that though it can be about marriage, it is not specific to marriage, or even primarily about marriage.

The text says that God creates the woman because it is not good for humanity to be alone, not because it is bad that humanity is unmarried. When the man sees the woman, he calls her "bone of bone and flesh of flesh" because she was made from something that was taken out of him. She is distinct, yet she comes from him.

This mysterious connection of two distinct entities made from different material yet formed by the same hand is such that the narrator can call it "one-flesh." The completion of humanity is called "bone of bone and flesh of flesh," and the complexity of humanity is called "one flesh." It is in this context of complex, complete unity that the narrator can describe the man and woman as "naked and unashamed."

When we look at the definition of "naked," or *aram* in Hebrew, we find that it is a simple word that means unclothed.[11] Not only is there no sexual sense in the lexical definition but there is also no sexual sense in how *aram* is used in other places in the Hebrew Scriptures.

The particular thing about "naked" in the garden is that it is paired with "unashamed." Now, there are places in the Hebrew Scriptures where "naked" is paired with shame. The prophets utilize the idea that the sin of the people causes them shame that is like being stripped naked before God and the nations. But for the prophets it is not the nakedness itself that is shameful. What is shameful is sin. We can get our heads around the idea of shame like nakedness. But the garden narrative speaks of "unashamed" nakedness.

We look up from our Bibles. What does this mean? What is naked and unashamed? What have we lost? Think about it enough, and it's not hard to identify that there is something that separates us from each other and makes us feel we need to somehow cover ourselves. Even in the presence of the most trusted friend, there is a thing that hinders us. It must be cleared away, let down. But it is never fully cleared away or let down. Naked and unashamed with each other is a thing we feel we could almost grasp, but we never do.

What would it be like to be naked and unashamed on the earth? What would it feel like to be united to nature? We feel a homesick pull to be more a part of it, as if something inside us knows what we have lost. We are drawn to it as if we could climb into it. We scale mountains and swim oceans and try to lose ourselves in forests of trees as if there is something we could surmount, or perhaps something we could be a part of, but there is always something that separates. We are mindful, we work on relationships, we experience nature. We remember somehow from

11. Brown, *Brown-Driver-Briggs Hebrew and English Lexicon*, 735.

deep within our center that encumbered is unnatural, but even so, naked and unashamed is foreign.

There is a flaming sword in each of us. Any advance meets reticence from inside and a steady force from outside. Foreign yet familiar, it does not yield. Dark ugly persistent push like a course hand on your chest.

A CRAFTY SERPENT, THE WOMAN, AND WISDOM

We have already noted that "*aram*" bears no sexual sense in other places in the Hebrew Bible.[12] It is a neutral word that means the state of being unclothed. But a word study is not the only way to get at the meaning of a mysterious word or phrase in Scripture. We can have a look at the images and ideas that accompany it in the pericope. When we do this, we find that the way the word "naked" is used in the garden narrative is more closely linked to ideas having to do with wisdom and knowledge than with marriage, sex, or even the state of being unclothed.

The original readers would have seen this readily, but since we do not read Hebrew, we do not. A look at the images surrounding nakedness involves that old serpent, the Hebrew word that describes him, and how women are connected with wisdom.

The "serpent" is a serpent. Later New Testament revelation and extra-biblical writing links the serpent with Satan. However, at this point in the story, the serpent is a serpent. He is a creature in the garden, a mystical and strange one, but a creature nonetheless. If for a moment we simply see the serpent as a serpent, we are unencumbered, and we can more readily accept that his presence would have tipped the ancient audience off that this pericope is about wisdom and knowledge.

---

12. Saul strips himself naked in 1 Sam 19:24. In Job 1:21 and Eccl 5:15 naked refers to nakedness at birth. Job 22 and 24 uses the word to mean without clothing. In Job 26 "Sheol is naked before God." Isaiah, Hosea, Amos and Micah speak of nakedness like the shame of sin.

Serpents in the Ancient Near East were associated with "sovereignty, life, fertility, wisdom, chaos and death."[13] Genesis describes the serpent as "shrewder" than any beast of the field which the Lord God had made"[14] The word for "shrewd, prudent or crafty" in Hebrew is *arum*. In Proverbs, *arum* describes a person who acts wisely or shrewdly. So, we have a serpent, who is a creature connected with wisdom, who is described as *arum*. The serpent asks the woman about things having to do with knowledge. It seems an obvious point, but I think it is often lost in interpretation that the serpent asks the woman about knowledge, not about sex or marriage. The tree is called the tree of the knowledge of good and evil.

Additionally, in Ancient Near Eastern understanding, the woman is associated with wisdom. The serpent addressed the woman not because she is easily beguiled or because the man is stupid but because serpents and women are both associated with wisdom.[15]

We discussed above that the Hebrew word *aram* means "naked." As we can see, the consonants that form *aram* and *arum* are the same, so the two words look almost identical in the Hebrew text. Ancient Jewish writers did this often. They would take two seemingly unrelated words that are formed from the same consonants like *aram* and *arum* and use them in the same pericope. This literary device creates a web of words that signals the reader that though they seem unrelated, the words should be thought of together because they illuminate each other.

The Hebrew word for naked, *aram*, looks and sounds like *arum*, the Hebrew word for "crafty, shrewd, sensible."[16] The serpent, who is more *arum* than any of the other creatures, promises humanity that they will be like God and know good and evil if they eat the fruit of the tree—so they do. However, instead of becoming wise, they become aware that they are *aram*, naked. They have

13. VanGemeren, *New International Dictionary of Old Testament Theology and Exegesis*, 85.

14. Gen 3:1.

15. Meyers, *Discovering Eve*, 91.

16. Brown, *Brown-Driver-Briggs Hebrew and English Lexicon*, 791.

indeed gained some sort of knowledge because they can now see that they are naked. However, instead of becoming more like God in knowledge and wisdom, the knowledge they have gained has made them less like God.

Before, they were naked; the identity and individuality of the man and of the woman was plain to see. Yet they were unashamed. There was no need to cover or protect this individuality, for it was a mysterious and awesome image of diversity unified. In this new wisdom, they know they are naked, but now they are ashamed.

What if ashamed nakedness in the garden is the realization of the loss of the complex unity that images God? Distinction without inhibition or competition is gone. The differences between how the woman was created and how the man was created were part of the complex thing meant to image the limitless God. Now they feed the ugly need for humanity to protect, hide, and hoard what was meant to be shared.

I will not think of you more than I must. The sword twists and moves. Do not listen. Do not see. Humanity is alone.

WHO IS FIRST?

Our second question has to do with how God created humanity. Common interpretation figures that hierarchy and humanity were created at the same time. The man is first; the woman is second. Hierarchy.

Much of this misunderstanding arises because the Hebrew word *adam* is usually translated as "man." But a much better translation is "humanity." Unlike English, Hebrew nouns are gendered. Gendered nouns are a grammatical, not a sexual, distinction. So, for instance, the noun for "temple" is feminine, and the noun for "song" is masculine. The noun for humanity is masculine, which is why the pronoun that follows it in Gen 1:27 is masculine, too. But this is grammatical.

Therefore, a better read is "God created *humanity* in his own image, in the image of God he created (humanity), male and female he created them." This translation is not based on a feminist need for equality, though it does reflect equality. This translation more accurately depicts the point that Gen 2–3 is about the creation of humanity, not the creation of hierarchy.

In other Ancient Near Eastern creation stories, the crowning achievement is created last. In the Genesis creation story, humanity is created last—God's image, God's great masterpiece. But as the story goes, the woman is the final work of the creation of humanity. She was made after the man.

Does this mean that the woman is the ultimate act of creation? Perhaps Gen 2–3 really is about a hierarchy God intended the woman to be at the top of. Why not? There is quite a celebration when she is created. God brings her to the man, eliciting a joyful exclamation from him. The narrator marks her creation with a little poem that speaks what will happen because of her. The man will leave his birth origin and be so committed to unity that the connection itself remembers how the hand of God created her.

This is quite compelling until we remember that this line of thinking is a great example of our discussion above. Thinking this way imposes the effects of the curse on the story before the story itself does.

The woman is not higher than the man. Instead, she completed God's process of creating humanity. When God created the woman, God finished the complex entity that is the image of the Godhead. Diversity and complexity is united in a fellowship born of differences that do not divide but strengthen. This encircling, protecting, strengthening thing mysteriously looks something like the God who created it.

Unity creates unity, and it is very good. Unity itself is God's ultimate work of creation. It is God's great masterpiece.

Hierarchy is so firmly entrenched in our thinking that we cannot help but swim in its influence. We cannot help but think of the order of creation. Who is created first? Does that mean he is higher? Who is created second? She is lower, or higher. But the creation of humanity is a process. No part of the process is more important than the other, especially when we imagine what the intended finished product was supposed to look like.

IT LOOKS LIKE TWO SIDES OF A WHOLE . . .

God took something out of the man to create the woman. We usually translate that something "rib." The Hebrew word is *tsela*. The garden is the only place in the Torah where the word *tsela* is translated "rib." Most everywhere else *tsela* has to do with the structure of the Ark of the Covenant or the Tabernacle of the Temple. *Tsela* is a symmetrical opposite side to something. For the Ark of the Covenant, *tsela* refers to the poles and rings that are placed symmetrically so that it can be carried. For the Temple, *tsela* refers to the opposite sides of the structure of the Tabernacle, like its walls or chambers.

God created the woman because he said that it was not good for humanity to be alone. The Hebrew word that is translated "alone" in Gen 2:18 is *bad*. This word is used repeatedly in the rest of the Torah for the poles (*bad*) on either side (*tsela*) of the Ark of the Covenant and the altar. The poles needed to be on perfectly symmetrical opposite sides so that the Ark and the altar could be carried level and not tip.

There are other places in the Torah where the word *bad* is used that do not have to do with the essential carrying poles for these sacred things. The word can mean a part of something that is separated from the whole. In Gen 21, the word describes the lambs Abraham separates from a flock. More significantly, in Deut 1, Moses explains to the people how he found he could not bear the burden of leading the people alone (*bad*) so he set up leaders over each tribe to lead with him. In Deut 8, Moses tells the people that they cannot live by bread alone (*bad*) but that physical bread is essentially accompanied by the word of God in order for the people to have life. When we look at these other uses in the Scriptures, we see that already, right from the start, when God saw that it was not good for humanity to be alone, God was clearly not looking for a mere sidekick for the first human. Right away, humanity was not complete, there was a whole that it was only a part of, and the rest of that whole must be created.

The finished product of humanity was the furthest thing from a hierarchy. It did not look at all like something that had one side higher than the other. On the contrary, humanity was built to be two perfectly symmetrical opposite-level sides. These images would have painted a clear picture to the ancient hearers of the garden story who were familiar with the Ark and the Temple.

Male and female are two equal, symmetrical sides of a whole that must balance each other perfectly or things will tip; things will be incomplete. Once unity is destroyed at the tree, essential things become crooked and do not work as they should. First, second, who is higher, who is lower have absolutely nothing to do with two balanced sides of the whole. This problem is as impactful as an Ark that slides off its uneven rails or a Temple split in two.

HELPER OR SIDEKICK?

Third, much has been made of the phrase in Gen 2:18 that describes the woman as a "helper" to the man.

The Hebrew word *ezer* is a noun that means "help." This help has largely been interpreted to mean that the woman is a little sidekick who is in a lower position to the man. However, when we look at how *ezer* is used in other places in the Hebrew Bible, we find that it most often describes the help of God. In Deuteronomy God is a help (*ezer*) against the adversaries of Judah; God rides through the heavens to be help (*ezer*); God is a shield of help (*ezer*) against enemies. The Psalms are loaded with images of God being help (*ezer*) for souls, for the poor, as a deliverer, for physical safety. The Psalms attribute this help to the power of the one who created the heavens and the earth, the love of the one who can bless those whose hope lies in this help.

The text is not saying that the woman is God, but it certainly is not relegating her "help" to the status of a sidekick either. When we think about this considering God's intention for humanity it makes perfect sense that the completion of humanity with the creation of the woman would somehow provide help to humanity like the help of God. If God exists in some sort of mysterious unity within the Godhead, God's image must exist in unity too. If there is fellowship in the Godhead, and if there is help between God and humanity, then it only follows that God's image was meant to be help for each other. Humanity's fellowship is meant to be like the deep connection within the Godhead and between God and humanity—help like the help of God.

What would it look like if we had the unity God intended? Any person we pass on the street is a person of deep value and connection, bone of bone and flesh of flesh. What would it look like if humanity was so united to each other, to God and to the earth that each person was help like the help of God to each other?

UNIQUE CHARACTERISTICS
AND THE DIVERSE UNITY

Now that we have distinguished some traditional interpretations from the actual words of Scripture, we are free to have a look at who the man and the woman are before the curse. It is at this point in our study when we remember that the coach is still a coach: it has not yet turned back into a pumpkin. We have established that to understand the biblical story, we must not impose the effects of the curse on our interpretation before the narrative does. We will look at these characteristics, understanding that they are manifested in the garden before the matter of the tree.

Something else to consider is that the characteristics the story attributes to the woman are descriptive, not prescriptive. They are given to the woman, but this does not mean that they are essentially feminine. We still have a coach, not a pumpkin. God gives these characteristics to complete the complex unity of humanity, not to mark out a division of what is masculine and what is feminine.

First, before God creates the woman, there is no such thing as human relationship. This seems obvious and even silly, but it is interesting to ponder. Before she is created, the man is alone. After she is created, there is relationship. Can we even say that she was created for relationship? After all, the woman is not created from the stuff of the ground, she is created from the stuff of humanity.

Now right away we could say this must mean that women are more relational than men. But when we do that, we are allowing our thinking to be colored by the disunity that happened in the wake of the curse, instead of pondering the unity that existed before the curse.

A second thing that happens after the woman is created is that humanity begins to wrestle with the word of God. If we look back at Gen 2:17, when God commands humanity not to eat from the tree of the knowledge of good and evil, we see that this command is given only to the man. The woman has not yet been created.

Now, the man is no passive resident of the garden. According to Gen 2:15, he cultivates and keeps it, and in Gen 2:20 he names all the animals. Active as the man is, he does not question or interact with the command of Gen 2:17. However, once God completes the creation of humanity with the woman, she begins to interact with the command. Before she is created, the command goes undiscussed. After she is created, humanity wrestles with it. Again, we would be wrong to conclude that women are more equipped to analyze and discuss the law than men are. Yes, the woman is the one who engages in the debate about the word of God, but the man is "with her."

What if, before the pronouncement of the curse in Gen 3, the differences between the man and the woman were not comparable, as if they were the possession of each individual sex? What if the characteristics we see in the man and in the woman were meant to be used together, in order that each would be a powerful help to the other? Gifts are meant to be thrown into the pot of one-fleshness so that they can be used together.

Here again, we are broadening what "one flesh" in the garden means. Yes, the "one flesh" of the man and the woman in the garden has been interpreted as a marital bond. Jesus himself interpreted it as such.[17] However, if we limit "one flesh" to marriage, we limit the idea that it can also refer to the contribution of both sexes in other settings. This idea seems foreign because after the garden, one flesh union has been corrupted, and our thinking about roles

17. Matt 19:6; Mark 10:8.

of men and of women have been influenced by that corruption. However, the special characteristics we see between the man and the woman are God's gifts given to all humanity.

Though the woman is made from the man and the man is made from the ground, all the children who will come from them will be of the ground and of the rib. Women and men are *humanity*. God calls the woman help like the help of God, but the man is the opposite, balancing side. He too is help like the help of God.

The female, humanity, is created for relationship. She is created to interact with God's command and to complete the human connection. The male, humanity, is created to be rooted in the good earth, the cultivator of the good of God, to care for it in such an intimate way as to name and form things of creation into more things of creation.

Humanity completes humanity. Humanity is made to cling to this unity. Gifts given to each are meant to be used by both for relationship, for good rule, for filling and ruling the earth with goodness like a garden. This is God's good intention.

CURSED DISUNITY

Like coming home to find home in ruin. Like seeing enough to remember how it once was—whole, how things are supposed to be. The foundation is in the ground, yet the structure is almost unrecognizable. Almost. The woman is still bone of bone and flesh of flesh. For the rest of human time, men will come from women, and women will come from men. But the green and gold garden warmth is breached, and the cold of the outside slaps. Men are born into struggle, and women are born into hiding. What God joined was never meant to be torn, but one flesh is torn and God's gifts spill out. The man and the woman grab them, claim them, pervert them. Unity disintegrates. Little shards fall away piece by piece. It is strange because it does not happen all at once. The man and the woman together have their eyes open, together see each other's nakedness, and together sew leaves to cover themselves. Together they hear the Lord walking in the garden, and together they hide. But the moment God finds them everything changes.

In Gen 1:28, God speaks to humanity and commands them to multiply, fill the earth, rule, and subdue it. Now, in Gen 3:9, Yahweh speaks again but only to the man. It is as if God is confirming what has just happened. It is as if God sees the separation of humanity and names it by speaking only to the man. When the man responds it is an affirmation of what God has spoken. Even though the man and the woman hid together in Gen 3:8, the man answers, "'I' heard the sound, 'I' was afraid because 'I' was naked so 'I' hid 'myself.'" It is as if the man is alone in the garden.

Why does God talk only to the man?

"Have you eaten from the tree of which I commanded you not to eat?" The man admits his guilt. "I ate." He does not say that he did not know what he was doing. He does not try to convince God that the woman forced him, tricked him, or beguiled him. But this is the first time in the conversation that the man includes the woman. His answer is an answer of unity. He includes God, himself, and the woman in his explanation of why he ate from the tree.

Finally, God turns to the woman. The action of the scene slows and darkens. Before this, God has asked the man a rapid fire of specific questions. For the man, the answers can be found easily in the facts of what has just happened, and they come as quickly as God's questions do. But when God turns to the woman, the question is deep and dark. There is more to this question than there was to the others. There is no objective answer, and God asks it to the woman alone. "What have you done?" Her answer is simple and incomplete. It touches only gingerly on the deep mysterious thing that has happened. The man's answer unites the man, the woman and God. But the woman answers herself alone with the serpent.

THE CURSE

We call what happened in the garden, "the curse." And I think that is a good name for it. "Curse" is the opposite of "bless" in both modern and biblical language. In the Bible, God is determined to bless humanity even though humanity routinely does things that bring about curse. It is important for us to note that God does not curse humanity. God curses the serpent and the ground. When God turns to the woman and to the man and speaks what will come of their disobedience, God tells each of them what will happen because "you have done this." Humanity has brought this trouble upon itself. God is simply naming it. Humanity curses humanity.

HELP LIKE THE HELP OF GOD

It is strange how God engages separately with the man and with the woman in the garden after the tree. It is the beginning of what we will see in the rest of the Genesis narrative. God is help to Abraham. Sarah is silent and in the background. God is help to Sarah. Abraham is silent and in the background. There are moments of unity between the men and the women of Genesis, things that distantly remember the garden, but they are rare. The women operate in their own little sphere, and the men operate in their own larger one. The whole walking together in the garden thing seems far away—so far away that we will wonder for the rest of our study whether the men and women of Genesis are even aware of the garden and what happened there. Do they even consider God's words of consequence?

Yet, even if humanity barely remembers, God remembers. The garden lives on the pages of the Bible. It seems the garden might live in God's heart, too. It is as if God loves the unity of the garden so much that God steps in to help the man in the place where the woman should have been. God invites Abraham to walk with him. God calls him to the same thing God called humanity to in the garden. Fill the land. Abraham is God's friend. God's word says it outright in Isa 41.

It is as if God loves the unity of the garden so much that God will step in to help Sarah in the place where Abraham should have been. God sees and hears Sarah. Sarah is beloved of God. God's word sings this belovedness almost imperceptibly. Almost. But it is there.

It is as if God loves the unity of the garden so much that God will work with humanity through all history to see his good intention through. God will have God's way. Unity is what God intended, and unity is what God is working towards. God must love the unity of the garden so much that God is willing to take the time and the pain to work together with fractured humanity to see God's good intention through.

Though the fracture is there, God bridges it with God's help. It seems strange and mysterious that God could stomach the pain it takes to work with humanity throughout all history and time. But God is determined to share. He is determined that humanity rule the ground and multiply the seed. But in the wake of the curse, God must help, because humanity fails miserably to be help for each other.

We look up from our Bibles, and we ponder for ourselves what the destruction of unity means. Is this why there is something of separation that exists between my heart and the heart of the one I love the most? Is this why I struggle to understand even myself sometimes, and why we agonize over our place in the world, and meaning, and actual, true love for others? It really does all go back to the garden, doesn't it?

When we see our own pain reflected in the story of the Bible, we hold it a little longer—turn it another time again—light, angle, color. We listen all the closer for the voice of the one who hears us and who sees us, just as God heard and saw Sarah long ago.

CHAPTER 3

Linekeepers and Landholders

THINGS CONTINUE OUTSIDE THE bounds of the wonderful garden. What should have been together—fill the earth together, rule the ground together—is strangely separated. The man and the woman divide their concerns and go about them alone. This separate thing grows hardy outside the garden. It loves the thorns and thistles.

The man works the ground God took him from. Instead of the ground yielding a spreading garden, it is the place of the serpent, so the man is burdened by its threat instead of being blessed by its bounty. Abraham will think about wells, boundaries, conquest, and his own safety. Sarah comes along with Abraham when God calls him, but she is silent and in the background. Abraham follows Adam in a line of what we will call Landholders—men concerned about the cursed ground.

But Sarah will think about the seed. Now, the seed is impacted by the serpent, too. Whatever that "enmity" God spoke of means, it is something dark between the seed of the woman and the seed of the serpent. Producing seed is toil, and the women in the Genesis narrative will struggle with their men and with each other to do it. Enmity.

Interestingly however, there is a fundamental difference between what God says to the man and to the serpent, and what God says to the woman. God's words of consequence foresee the serpent's crawl, the man's return to the dust, and the woman's pain. But embedded in God's word to the serpent, God speaks hope to the woman. She is the only one of the three whose consequences involve hope. Somehow, her seed will crush the head of the serpent. Somehow the seed of the woman will have something to do with destroying what is cursed. In the story of the Bible, the seed God promises becomes a line, and the line becomes the family of Israel. Grow the seed. Keep the line. The men might hold the land, but the women grow the seed. We will call these women Linekeepers.

We know these Linekeepers well. They are women the likes of Rebekah who came after Sarah. Like Abraham before her she agreed to go to a place she did not know. She lived in her mother-in-law's tent—a comfort to Isaac. She continues what Sarah began. Rebekah is barren too, and in a little remembrance of the unity of Eden, Isaac comes before God to ask for a child for her. God gives them two.

The Linekeepers are Leah weak and Rachel beautiful, who contend with each other and with Jacob and with God to build the tribes of Israel. Tamar cleverly sees the tribe of Judah through despite Judah's recklessness. And when those tribes find themselves in deadly Egypt, the Linekeepers are mighty protectors. They lie and cover and scheme and endanger themselves for the seed. The midwives stand before the face of Pharaoh and declare the women of Israel strong because they refuse to endanger the seed. Moses' mother and sister change the course of the fate of Israel by protecting baby Moses. Miriam stands before the face of Pharaoh's daughter and enlists her in this work of protection too and the great deliverer of Israel is nursed in the arms of his own mother.

We turn and ponder these Linekeepers—light, angle, color. If we look behind the wars and wells and wandering of the Landholders, we find the machinations of the Linekeepers. The stories of the men are at the forefront of the narrative. They are the ones God's name reflects—the God of Abraham, Isaac, and Jacob. The men move their families to key places for key things to happen. At first read, it seems the women only come along, essential because they bear and rear the children. But the stories of the women wind in and out of the action and form a structure that prioritizes the heart of the matter, the protection of the line. They are the rib that encircles.

We cannot tell if the women after Eve are thinking about the time in the garden and God's word of hope. It does not seem so. Neither the men nor the women mention the garden. They do not talk about the old serpent and how God promised that a seed from the woman would crush its head. The matriarchs and patriarchs do not reflect on what that crushed head might mean, how ultimately what humanity tore apart God would repair and how the one who would come from the seed would heal the land and everything else too. That all comes later as the story of the Bible unfolds. Even so, the seed of these things seems somehow to lie in the hearts of the Linekeepers. It seems so because of what the Linekeepers *do*.

When we think about what the Linekeepers do in the narrative, we have to wonder if it is possible there is something about the woman on the outside of the garden that remembers where she came from on the inside of it. Something about her action somehow remembers that she was taken from humanity itself. Something remembers the inside place God's hand formed her from, the help God created her to be, and that hope God spoke to the woman. Is it possible that something from deep within their center moves her to protect the line?

We discussed in chapter one how the significance of the characters' actions may fly higher than what any individual character understands at the time and place of their action. The word of God portrays something we see only when we stand back and look at the entire story. The Linekeepers are an example of this. They do dangerous and decisive things to protect the line. Think about how they deal with two Pharaohs, for instance. Sarah agrees to enter one Pharaoh's harem, and the midwives, Miriam, Moses' mother, and Pharaoh's own daughter defy another right under his nose. Their protective action is too decisive to be arbitrary. Perhaps it is a combination of things, a mixture of conscious and unconscious motivation. But the Linekeepers are driven by something—that at least seems certain.

I think there are two hints in the text worth pondering as we wrestle with their motivation. First, the "desire" God speaks of, and second, the fact that God speaks to humanity at all in the first place.

DESIRE

We talk a lot about what it means for the woman to be "ruled over," but God says some other things to humanity in the garden. What is this "desire?" When we read the story and observe the goals of the Linekeepers, the word "desire" seems to be a good but extremely complex descriptor.

The text says that the woman's desire will be for the man. This too has been interpreted to have something to do with sex. However, if we consider that the garden is more about the break of unity than it is about sex, we might consider a more multifaceted interpretation of "desire."

There are three places where the word translated "desire" is used in the Hebrew Scriptures. The first is in Gen 4:7 when God speaks to Cain. God tells Cain that the sin crouching at Cain's door "desires" him and that he must master it. In Song of Songs the word refers to sexual desire. The "desire" of Gen 3 is more challenging to define than the other two, but the other two uses of the word might help us to get at what "desire" means in Gen 3. Something of love? Something that crouches in wait? We might hold these two ideas as we think about the "desire" God prophesied about the woman. However, unlike these two uses that seem rather clear-cut, the "desire" in Gen 3 resists sharp definition.

There is an echo between the desire of the woman that will be ruled over by the man, and sin's desire for Cain that he must rule over. We hear this echo readily because both verses contain the same Hebrew words for "desire" and for "rule." Since they are so close together in the narrative, we might consider how they inform each other. The woman will desire her husband, yet he will rule over her. Sin will desire Cain, yet Cain must rule over it. To make things more pondersome, the word for "rule" in these two verses is the same word God uses when God calls humanity to rule the earth and to subdue it.

We have already discussed how the break of unity in the garden perverted humanity's rule. Clearly, man's rule over the woman is outside God's intention for humanity. However, the narrative also seems to be connecting the woman's desire that will be ruled over by the man with the sin of Cain that he must rule over.

Is the woman's desire like sin? Can we draw so tight a parallel between the woman's desire for the man and sin's desire for Cain? Or is the desire of the woman something neutral or even good that the man will seek to suppress? Does the desire of the woman become like sin as humanity becomes more and more violent, more and more determined to rule in a corrupt way in the shadow of the tree?

Either way—or some completely other way—we must not pin down the meaning of desire too tightly. As we continue to study Sarah and think about how desire and corrupted rule work in her life, we are better to hold things loosely than to sharply define them.

The tension between the desire of the woman and the rule of the man just brings more questions. The woman will desire her husband, and he will rule over her. How complex is this desire? Does she desire his rule? We can hardly read the story and not consider this. For the Linekeepers, desire to have and to protect the seed is strong—strong as the love of a beloved, and strong as something crouching in wait. Even though the curse says that the man will rule over the woman, when it comes to producing or protecting the seed the Linekeepers wield story-changing power. She is the rib that encircles, and she can wind her desire around whatever she sets her mind to. Does this threaten the man?

He takes centuries and times and places, all cultures, and every single language and his action takes only a small part of his vast strength. After all, he is bigger and stronger. His domain is the ground where every human must walk. The ground is the place of the serpent, the place of the promise of toil and the place the man returns. The ground is his home. He clings to it.

His promises are mundane and connected to the hard earth. Her promises are greater. They speak hope. Does something inside men push against this uneven distribution, this tipping? Grab, hide, hoard. Her body is the domain of the seed, a fertile place for God's hope. The man only has the ground. But he can rule it. The woman is smaller. It is not hard for his hand to push her down. Does he do this because he senses her height?

Does she?

The woman turns away from the garden and the flaming sword. She walks the dusty road silent to a place she does not know. Something terrifying obscures something good but still something remains.

TALKING TO GOD

God speaks into humanity's days. He speaks things that must be done or that will come to pass. God speaks love constant, love unrequited, pain experienced, pain understood.

God talks to kings, but usually he does that through a prophet. When God talks to Eve, Sarah, and Rebekah it is intimate and close from the God who knows and sees to a woman who hears and acts. Not all the Linekeepers have talks with God. Or maybe they do; it is just that the story of the Bible does not include them. But Eve, Sarah, and Rebekah surely do. More than that, we know they recognize the importance of these talks because they respond with action. I suppose this itself is a thing to ponder. The fact that God's words come to pass is not the question that drives the story of the Bible. The question is what humanity does with the little stabs God's voice makes into history.

When we look at the action of the Linekeepers, we should balance three things in our minds: the word of hope God spoke to the woman in the garden, desire, and what God says to Eve, Sarah and Rebekah. This is because there is something going on between God and the Linekeepers. There is a particular sort of communication between them that has to do with the promise of the seed. If we think of these things when we observe what the women do, it helps us to see them as more than flat characters who piously seek the word of God or more likely as selfish troublemakers bent on their own goals. They are responding to a talk with God.

God speaks to the woman in the garden and tells her that childbearing will involve toil—and that her relationship with the man will involve corrupted rule. But God's word of hope stitches God and the woman together. Toil comes from childbearing and corrupted rule comes from the man, but the hope of the seed comes from God. The woman might answer herself alone with the serpent, and her desire might be perilously complex, but God is help. Gen 4:1 says that the man had "relations with his wife Eve," but Eve herself says that she has her baby boy because of the help of God. Genesis 4:25 says that Adam had relations with his wife "again," but again Eve gives God the credit for the birth of her son.

When Seth is born, Eve echoes God's word of hope again. Cain threatened the survival of the seed by killing his brother, Abel. But Eve says that God "appointed another seed." Eve herself names Seth to remember what God did for her. The name "Seth" is a word play on how God set Seth as the seed to replace Eve's lost sons. Grow the seed. Keep the line.

Sarah is the next developed women after Eve. Sarah is barren. If there is anyone whose hope hangs on God's help it is Sarah. And she gets it. God comes to the tent in the middle of the day in Gen 18 to prophesy "for Sarah a son." God is the one who can open and close wombs, and God can speak hope into the life of the hopeless woman. Somehow at some point old Abraham had relations with his wife too, but in Gen 21:6, after the baby boy is born, Sarah attributes the miracle to God.

Sarah goes further. She casts out Ishmael and his mother so that there is no threat to Isaac's inheritance. Is this unthinking and impetuous? Or is Sarah enacting just what God has said? Isaac is the line, not Ishmael. What God says matters.

Rebekah is barren, too. So "Isaac prayed to the Lord on behalf of his wife, because she was barren; and the Lord answered him and Rebekah his wife conceived" (Gen 25:21). But when the babies wrestle together in Rebekah's womb, Rebekah talks to God about it. God tells her that the older child growing in her will serve the younger. All Rebekah's actions that follow remember these words. She sees to it that they come to pass. Rebekah schemes so that Jacob, not Esau, is blessed. Jacob is the line, not Esau. God prophesies it, and Rebekah sees it through.

When God says something "shall" happen—that the woman shall bear a seed, or the promised child shall be the line to move God's plan, or one twin shall prevail over the other—the women see to it that the word God speaks is the word they do. Does Sarah do what she does because she is a trouble-making seductress like Eve before her? Do her sexual wiles and her lack of faith lead poor Abraham into folly? Or does Sarah do what she does because of a talk with God?

We do not know if God talks with Rachel, Leah, Tamar, or the midwives. The text does not say. We do not know if any of them are thinking about that word of hope to the woman in the garden. But Rachel and Leah contend with each other to produce sons for Jacob, and they name them to remember the help of God. The sisters compete using those sons, and they negotiate using Jacob, and from these games comes the flourishing of the line. They multiply Jacob and create the twelve tribes.

Tamar is willing to become a single mother to continue the line of Judah. Her disguise and lie prospers Judah's line. He did not ask for a son, but Tamar gives him two. The one named Perez continues the line of Judah, and the other named Zerah, or "seed" closely follows. The line of the seed survives because of Tamar, not Judah.

The Linekeepers continue into Exodus. The Hebrew midwives are not protecting their own children, instead they risk their necks to protect Israel. It is only as a reward from God that they have their own children. Seems a strange reward in a time when mothers are hiding children, but that is another thing entirely. The daughters of Israel protect the sons of Israel, and the promised seed grows. Miriam manipulates an Egyptian princess when she finds the hidden baby, and Moses is saved to someday save the line.

Grow the seed. Keep the line. Are they responding to a talk with God? We do not know. Are they thinking about that word of hope? The text does not say. Are they sweet women piously striving to do right by God and humanity? It does not seem so.

The ruled-over-ness of desire only highlights the strength of the desire. The strength of desire makes us wonder what is behind it. Desire strong and complex, ruled over and put down, but something like beloved love or maybe something crouching yet unmastered, it survives even on thorny ground.

Hide babies. Hide the barren woman. Blood hidden heard. Cries from palace halls and a hidden laugh. Disguise one child and cast out the other. Cast out one child and the other is the only one you see.

We turn now to Sarah, the mother of nations, the Linekeeper after the mother of the living, and the mother of the Linekeepers who will follow. Now that we have established her place in the shadow of the garden, she is the one we will study from here on. We have thought about who the woman was and who the woman became. We have thought about desire, help, talks with God, shame like nakedness, uneven dark tipping, and the cataclysmic break of unity. Great destruction followed the cataclysmic break of unity.

We turn now and ponder Sarah, and we must think about all these things. They are the background colors we look for and the leitmotif we lean in to hear. Sarah's laughter happens within Sarah's story, so we must understand that laughter within that story because it is more than the moment she laughed it.

Now imagine Sarah begins to think about the seed the day God comes to her tent to talk to her, to ask where she is and to hear her hidden laughter and to say that she really did laugh and to say, "For Sarah a son."

PART TWO

CHAPTER 4

So That It May Go Well with Me Because of You

WE HAVE HEARD OF Sarah before we find her on the road into Egypt. We have heard how Abraham brought her with him when God called him to go to a place he did not know. We have read her genealogy—or lack of one. They seem to be small details, how Sarah goes along with Abraham, and how she really has no genealogy. But these are keys to understanding Sarah.

When we first hear of Sarah, her name is Sarai, and she stands next to a woman named Milcah in the genealogy of Gen 11. Milcah is an undeveloped character in the rest of the narrative. The genealogy tells us about her family line, so it is strange that it tells us nothing about Sarah's. Right after we hear notably nothing about Sarah's history, we hear something essential about her future. "Sarai was barren, she had no child."

Sarah is distinct in her lack of distinction. She has no parentage and no children. She is not even set apart among the people Abraham brings from his home country to go to the land God promises him. The narrative mentions Lot first, and when it gets around to Sarah she is lumped in with another mention of Lot.

These things mean something about Sarah. When we make the error of separating them from the rest of the story, we might explain Sarah's lack of distinction by guessing that barrenness isolated a woman from community "back in Bible times." That might be true, but the narrative does not say anything about this. Instead, we get closer to the meaning of Abraham's request if we ground it in the story itself. When we do this, we recognize what the narrative is doing. Sarah's marginalized status is part of the story.

Abraham and Sarah are the next developed couple after Adam and Eve. They arise out of the line of men and women who stand in the shadow of the tree and who vividly depict how piece by piece unity falls apart. It is as if God's word is pointedly painting a picture of what happens when unity disintegrates. What has "bone of bone and flesh of flesh" become? The line of couples who stand between Adam and Eve and Sarah and Abraham tell us.

Cain's wife is distinct in her lack of distinction, too. She has no name. She births a son for Cain, but there is no record of anything she says or anything that is said to her. Cain names the city he builds "after the name of his son." The narrative repeats the word "name" to highlight that Cain, Cain's son Enoch, and the city all have names, but Cain's wife does not. Lamech's wives do have names—Adah and Zillah. But they do not have voices. They wordlessly take in Lamech's violent talk. Noah's wife is nameless and voiceless. Noah's story is well-developed, but his wife's is not. She is silent and in the background. The tear grows deep.

Here we stop and ponder. Sometimes we read the Bible story for story and fail to see the background colors that tie it all together. When we first meet Sarah on the road into Egypt, it is essential that we see her within the flurry of wretched women who follow Eve. When we see Sarah within this disaster and as a picture of this disaster we begin to understand. Abraham's request is nestled among these things of destruction. Is Sarah to Abraham what she is in the narrative, barren backwards and forwards, nameless and wordless? Does it mean anything to Abraham to endanger her? Is this what help like the help of God is reduced to? Sarah does not look anything like the woman in the garden.

We stand on that road into Egypt and watch Sarah. These things swirl in the air around us. We try to grasp them and turn them, for they are all we know about her at this point in the story.

What happens inside Sarah when Abraham's request hits her chest? Abraham's "please" implies that Sarah has some sort of agency in the situation. The text does not tell us, so we do not know. But Abraham does ask her. Although we do not hear her answer, she goes. Why does she go?

It means something that Abraham asks this of Sarah, and it certainly means something that she does it. What the situation in Gen 12 does not mean is that we can justify Abraham's request because things like selling your wife into another man's harem might have been part of the culture. We must abandon that line of thinking. It is belittling to Sarah and dismissive of what happened to her. Really when it comes down to it, we cannot assume this practice was common in the time and place of Abraham and Sarah anyway. Even if it was, it is still horrible. Either way, for the purposes of our study, we will interact with Sarah's time in Egypt not as a cultural glitch but as a key to understanding the patterns it creates in the story that surrounds it.

Sarah's laughter happens within Sarah's story. It is not isolated to the moment she laughs it. The moment we find Sarah on the road into Egypt and her time in Pharaoh's harem are significant to Sarah's laughter later in the story. First, Sarah's time in Egypt establishes Sarah as a protector and help. Second, Sarah's time in Egypt sets a precedent that begins with Sarah and will continue throughout the generations that come from her. God hears and helps her, and he will hear and help her children. Finally, Sarah's protective action in Egypt is illuminated and broadened in the story of Joseph.

SARAH PROTECTOR

Sarah is on the road into Egypt. There is a famine, and Abraham the Landholder is afraid of the land. He thinks Egypt will be better. After all, the famine in the land God promised is "severe." Perhaps

Egypt will be a refuge. But Abraham is afraid of Egypt too. He is certain Sarah's beauty will endanger him. He is afraid of the land, and he is afraid of its people, and he is afraid of Sarah's beauty. Really though, Abraham has nothing to fear because Sarah will protect him.

The very first thing Abraham says to Sarah begins with a "please." Perhaps he knows what he asks is something significant. Please allow me to endanger you so that it may go well with me. Now, the word of God contradicts the words of Abraham. The genealogy in Gen 11 bears no hint that Sarah is Abraham's sister, the daughter of his father but not his mother. Please lie.

Abraham takes the one he should have clung to and gives her away. Eden is far away. Help like the help of God asked to what?! Bone of bone and flesh of flesh in the hands of another man so that Pharaoh's hands treat Abraham well. Does Abraham think about Pharaoh's hands?

Sarah does it. She agrees. Why in the world does Sarah agree?

We look up from our Bibles, and we think about Sarah. How far is she from what God intended for her? Is unity's tear so deep and so pervasive that Sarah cannot conceptualize the destruction his request and her acquiescence signals? What is going on inside Sarah's heart that allows her response to Abraham's "please"? She does it. She agrees. But why?

The word of God does not tell us, so we do not know, but one slight turn of the prism brings a new question. Is it possible Sarah is closer to the garden than we think? Is there something to how God made the woman and what he made humanity to do for each other that moves Sarah to action? Is there something deep within her center that persists and pulls Sarah to protect?

We go back to the garden and consider how God created the woman. God took something from within humanity to complete humanity. This something is the perfectly symmetrical opposite side of the first human such that when God took from the one whole person, God created a new whole—something separate, but something a part of. Diversity unified. And this diversity unified is something protective like God's help so that humanity would be help like the help of God for each other.

But Sarah and Abraham are not in the garden. Help and unity are broken. Here we must think about how what was meant to be is severed. The coach is now a pumpkin. The shadow of the garden is a place where men and women divide their concerns. We can see the rift right there before us. Abraham thinks about famine, where to go, and how to protect himself. He is doing just what the curse said he would—toil on the ground. Famine is behind him, Egypt looms ahead of him, and Abraham is afraid of death.

We stand back a few paces on this road into Egypt and watch Sarah do exactly what Abraham asks her to do. Past interpretation glides over this moment, but it is very important. Sarah's action reflects God's intention—she is help. Her action also reflects the curse. She is doing exactly what the curse said she would. Is Sarah's desire for her husband so complex that she is willing to endanger herself? Is Sarah's concern for the promised seed as deep as Abraham's fear of the ground? Grow the seed. Keep the line.

Desire is something to cling to. Grab, hold, hide, hoard. It is something torn, weak tatters fall away as quickly as they can be grasped until the grasping exceeds the falling away and a small handful remains tight. Something to hold deep. Something to protect.

God's intention for humanity's help is terribly perverted. Yet, Sarah is help to Abraham. Sarah should not be in the position to help her husband by allowing herself to be prostituted in Egypt and Abraham should not be on the road out of the land God has just promised him. But despite the corruption of unity that would have kept Abraham from selling Sarah into the house of Pharaoh in the first place, Sarah maintains some semblance of how the woman was made—from and for a protective place, help like the help of God.

We cannot know what went through Sarah's mind when Abraham asked her to protect him, but we can look at the text and see what happened. Whether or not Sarah the person understands the significance of what she is doing, the meaning of her actions fly higher than her own experience. The words live on the page.

With a touch, shards tear and seams like bones remain. The man built from the land and for the land is afraid of the land. Can Sarah see his nakedness?

Like one clawing from the bottom of a pit, Sarah should not be in this spot. But the reality of the situation is that she is. The perfectly symmetrical opposite side has betrayed her. What should have been something of humanity's help for humanity only remembers the garden from a parched and thorny, deep, and desolate place. But even from this parched place, Sarah is effective.

If Abraham is correct, Pharaoh would have killed him on account of his wife, yet because Sarah protects him, Abraham lives. More than that, Abraham prospers. Pharaoh gives Abraham enormous wealth on account of Sarah. Interestingly, the very next story after Sarah in Egypt tells of how Abraham and Lot have to separate because of all their possessions and how Abraham is powerful enough to defend Lot against a coalition of kings. Was he this powerful and secure when he entered Egypt with Sarah? Or did Pharaoh give so generously that it changed Abraham's entire status? If so, the rib that encircles not only protected his life but also provided great physical security for him. It really does go well for Abraham because of Sarah.

GOD HEARS

The second observation we can make of Sarah's time in Egypt is that it continues a pattern that begins at the beginning of Genesis. We are so familiar with this pattern that we might take it for granted if we are not careful.

Here is another place to stop and think about how we read the Bible. We usually skip around and read one story here and apply another story there. But for the purpose of our study, we want to think about reading the narrative in order. We read this pericope about Sarah as if we have read straight through from the garden to here and as if we have not read further. We read as if we are only just now hearing the story. The reason this is so important is because the story is slowly establishing for us who God is. If we read in order, as if we do not know the next thing that is coming, and as if we do not know how it has been interpreted in the past, we see with fresh eyes that we are being introduced to God.

From the start, we discover that Yahweh is a God whose hands create and who walks like and with humanity in the garden. But there is something else we come upon if we are reading the story in order. We realize that God hears in ways that are unique to God and impossible for humanity. This pattern begins with Abel, continues with Sarah, and grows with the generations that will come from her.

Something terrible happens to Abel. Cain lures him out to the field and kills him. Abel never says a word in the narrative, he is completely silent. But as if it has a voice, Abel's blood cries out from the ground. And as if it has a will, it cries directly to God as if the blood knows God will listen. Unhearable things seek their way to God's ears.

Something terrible happens to Sarah too. Sarah silent on the road finds herself in Pharaoh's harem. Abraham is safe and Sarah is . . . we do not know, but Sarah in Egypt continues the pattern Abel's blood begins.

The road is silent and dusty in the still heat of the day. Sarah hears her breath, hears Abraham's, hears the sound of walking like trudging through thick fearful air. Silent. Silence. Does God ever cry out? Cry like the pain of a mother. Cry like blood in the ground. Cry like a lonely woman. Violence like a surprise. Pain like a gasp. Rage like a plague.

HEARING THE UNHEARABLE

As the story goes, the first time God talks to Abraham is when he calls him in Gen 12. God tells Abraham that he will give him a land and a people and the promise of blessing so that Abraham will be a blessing. If Sarah is there, she is silent and in the background.

The first time we hear a word from Abraham, he is taking a thing or two up with God. He is worried. Even though God promised Abraham a great family, he fears a servant, not a son, will inherit his household. Again, if Sarah is there, she is silent.

Abraham's first word to Sarah is his "please." Please, so that it may go well with me. But through all this, Sarah is silent. She silently goes with Abraham to the new land; she silently goes with Abraham when he decides to go into Egypt. Sarah silently agrees to Abraham's "please," and she silently enters Egypt. But I think her silence ends there.

The text does not tell us, so we do not know how long Sarah was in Pharaoh's palace. Did the cool halls and intricate mosaics become familiar to her? Was there a time her confusion ceased in the pitch darkness of the middle of the night? Where am I? Oh, yes. Or was Sarah in Egypt less than twenty-four hours? We do not know.

What we do know is that God got her out of there. As the story goes, God "touched Pharaoh and his house with great plagues." The reason God did this was because of "the word of Sarah." Now, most translations read "because of Sarah." I don't know why this is. The Hebrew is quite clear—"The Lord touched Pharaoh and his house with great plagues on account of the word of Sarah" (Gen 12:17).

The very first word Sarah says in the narrative is a word to God from Egypt. If we could enter the cool halls of Pharaoh's palace and move silently into the room where Sarah sleeps, we would not hear her word any more than we could hear blood cry from the ground or hear Sarah laugh if we slipped silently into a corner of her tent to listen on that day God came to tell her she would have a son. But what if, sure as a cry of blood from the ground and laughter laughed deep inside seek God's ears, Sarah's word from Egypt seeks God's ears too?

If we are reading the story in order and learning about God as we go, Abel's cry that God uniquely hears is still on our minds. If we continue reading into Exodus, Israel's time in Egypt reminds us of Sarah's time in Egypt. We hear about how Israel cries out to God from slavery and how God hears and acts by touching Pharaoh with plagues. This is the same thing God did for Sarah. Even though God responded to Sarah's "word" and God responded to Israel's "cry" by sending plagues, the connection is so clear you could call Sarah's word a type to Israel's cry. Sarah appeals to God from Egypt sure as her children do generations later. God hears and protects them sure as God heard and protected their mother. God protects and delivers Sarah to reenter the promised land sure as God will protect and deliver her children to reenter generations later. It is the same thing. God is a God who hears and helps. This is true right from the start with Abel and Sarah and it continues with all the children who would come from her.

This I suppose is the kind of thing that throws different kinds of light depending upon where we stand, what we have done to others and what others have done to us. Things like these are meant to be kept so that they may be pulled out and thought about some more. We ponder Sarah's silence, her word become cry, her laughter. What is inside it? What is the meaning of a perfectly symmetrical opposite side? And what is the extent of the damage that happens to the soul when it betrays? And in our own silences, our own words become cries, our own complex laughter—is God a God who hears?

If God is our Mother Father, and if God is bound up in us, does God feel pain for Sarah like a woman feels pain for her child? Read the Scriptures enough and you can hear God's pain. The Scriptures are not silent about God's pain.

We look up from our Bibles. It does not take long to know what it feels like to be hurt by someone who should have been help. Walk long enough on this earth, and the idea of relationship without opposition is something we can barely conceptualize here on this side of what we call the curse, this torn apart thing, this humanity hurting humanity thing. But it seems we must pause a bit and think about Sarah in the cool halls of Pharaoh's palace and how perhaps she cried out to God. At the very least we must pause and think about her pain. Whether or not her experience was common in her time, it had to have been empty and hurtful, scary, and disorienting.

When we ponder the pain in her story, we can think about our own experiences, and we can consider new things—things like how Sarah speaks a word out of the long silence that began with the women before her, and how God hears it and springs into action to deliver her. When we ponder the pain in the story, we can think about how Sarah laughs an unhearable laugh from a hidden place and God hears it. "Yes, you did laugh." The meaning behind our own complex responses to things, our own complex laughter, is hidden to us sometimes too.

The Hebrew word for "cry" and the Hebrew word for "laugh," when spoken, sound almost the same. This Sarah story that begins with her word become cry, her hidden laugh, begins a whole chain of cries and laughs hearable and unhearable, complex and simple, clear and misunderstood. Sometimes to us, all this can become noise and can sound the same to the untrained ear. But the story is telling us that God hears us like he hears Sarah, differently and uniquely, intimately and with deep perception.

If we think about it this way, Sarah's word swirls in the air like something waiting to be planted and to grow. It points ahead to the cries of her seed hundreds of years later from that same place. It points even further ahead to Sarah's seed like stars of the sky and sands of the seashore who cry out from all times and in all places. Sarah's word remembers that God hears one barren woman in one time and in one desolate place. But in the same way her word remembers the cry of each person in each place. For humanity has created desolation for itself everywhere.

Something small as a word bursts forth like a laugh—or a cry— like a gasp in. A cry begins simple as a word. Something realized like something dawning. Rebellion? Advocacy? Who knows? Hear me. Do not throw me away.

SARAH AND JOSEPH

Our final observation about Sarah in Egypt has to do with the connection between Sarah and Joseph. There are multiple parallels in the narrative that signal to us that each story informs the other.

Joseph is the son of Jacob and Rachel, the grandson of Isaac and Rebekah, the great-grandson of Abraham and Sarah. The Joseph narrative is the longest treatment in Genesis of any single character other than Abraham. Readers of Scripture have wondered about this. Why devote so much space to one person, even if his story is compelling and unique, and even if it establishes the reason the twelve tribes end up in Egypt? Joseph's story has many purposes, but we will consider how Joseph's story in Egypt is a picture of Sarah's story in Egypt.

In some ways, we could look at Joseph as a Linekeeper also. After all, he actively protects and prospers the line of Israel. Without Joseph's massive food program, the twelve tribes (and much of the ancient world for that matter) would have perished. Instead of calling him a Linekeeper however, we will consider how his story points to Sarah as a Linekeeper.

The Joseph narrative shows us in magnitude what we first see in simplicity in Sarah's. It is bigger than Sarah's, and Joseph's effect seems to be broader. Sarah's action is small. She protects Abraham. Joseph's action is huge. He saves the twelve tribes, Egypt, and Canaan.

However, Joseph's wide scope points ahead to Sarah's much wider scope. Joseph helps for seven years, but the blessing that eventually comes from Sarah's seed will be available for all time. Joseph's action saves some. He stores up "grain in abundance, like the sand in the sea" (Gen 41:49). Sarah's action saves the father of Israel so that the seed of Israel can produce people as "countless as the stars and as numerous as the sands on the seashore" (Gen 22:17).

JOSEPH AND SARAH . . .

Joseph is alone. When did the realization of the full extent of his brothers' hatred hit his heart? They pull him up. Hope. They sell him to Egypt. Betrayal. A deep wound inflicted at close range. His past is far away with his father. His future is certainly gone. He is barren—cut off. Even when Joseph finds himself in the bright house of

Pharaoh with a coat of power and a ring of status, he remains the lost son. He tells himself that he has forgotten home, yet he names his children for his homesickness.

Sarah is barren backwards and forwards. No past. The genealogy is silent about her. The first thing the word of God says about Sarah is that she is barren. No future. Motherless and fatherless and childless. Do not listen, do not see. Throw her away.

Joseph's brother Judah repeats the sin of his great-grandfather Abraham. Judah, protected and prospered, sells his own brother—bone of bone and flesh of flesh—into Egypt. Unlike Sarah, Joseph is not silent. Later in the story the brothers themselves remember how frightened Joseph was and how frantically he begged them to not do what they were going to do.

The brothers are jealous. That is why they throw Joseph away. Abraham is what? Heartless? Clueless? We do not know. But what we do know is that the parallels between Sarah and Joseph begin with prophecies that come to pass.

One comes quickly. Joseph's dreams of his family, like sheaves and stars bowing down, come true within years of Joseph dreaming them. His brothers come in need to Egypt. They stand before him full of fear of what the land can do to them and hunger for what it has already done. They bow before this brother of theirs hidden behind the guise of Egyptian royalty. "The dreamer" has a name second only to Pharaoh's.

Sarah's prophecy is still coming to pass to this day. Sarah hidden and barren becomes Sarah mother of nations. Stars in the sky like sands on the seashore are not just for Abraham. God reverses Sarah's status sure as Pharaoh reversed Joseph's, but Sarah's stars and sand have no end.

Sarah's beauty is a problem. It is dangerous, Abraham reasons. So that it will go well for Abraham, and so that Abraham will live and not die, he sells his beautiful wife into Egypt. And it does go well for Abraham.

As the story goes, it is a bit the same and a bit different for Joseph. Different, because Joseph does not agree—he was never asked—to go into Egypt. The same, because Joseph and Sarah are both called "beautiful" in Genesis. We are sure Sarah's beauty is the problem. Abraham says it outright. But Joseph's beauty might be a problem too. The brothers are jealous. The story says it outright. They are jealous of their father's uneven love for Joseph, they are jealous of his dreams—sheaves and stars bowing before this beautiful boy. Perhaps they are jealous of his beauty too. Beauty is not always a blessing. Ask Sarah.

The two beautiful ones sold into Egypt by bone of bone and flesh of flesh are unprotected protectors. It really does go well for the brothers because of Joseph. Unlike their great-grandfather Abraham, they do not anticipate this, but Joseph's time in Egypt saves their lives as sure as Sarah's time saves Abraham's.

Each story echoes and points to the other. There is silver for the brothers when Joseph is enslaved in, silver and gold for Sarah's husband when she is freed out. God protects the son of the father's old age sure as God protects the woman who would bear a son in hers. Though Pharaoh commands his forces concerning her, it is God who frees Sarah. Though Pharaoh elevates Joseph, it is God who is with him. Pharaoh will command troops concerning the twelve tribes when they come out of Egypt too, and again, God will protect and prosper. Abraham will conquer kings in the land and his descendants will conquer cities.

There are two "severe" famines strangely dissimilar. It seems Sarah's famine does not last long. We don't know this, but her time in Egypt seems quick. Joseph's famine is enormous. It is pervasive. It stretches through all Egypt, to Canaan, and through the entire known world. It is complete. It lasts seven years.

There are two Pharaohs strangely alike. Both Pharaohs listen and readily respond to the praise people around Joseph and around Sarah speak. Neither Pharaoh worships Yahweh, but both are quick to fear this foreign God. Sarah's Pharaoh somehow knows the plagues are because of Sarah and from God. He immediately provides not only an escort for Abraham and Sarah out of Egypt but riches for Abraham. Joseph's Pharaoh somehow knows that Joseph's wisdom is from God. He too is quick to elevate Joseph to power second only to himself.

These two good Pharaohs foreshadow one deeply evil one, a man with a hardened heart who hardens his heart to love death. He will come generations after Sarah's and Joseph's Pharaohs, but he looms in the background of their stories. The plagues from God that free the first beautiful one foreshadow the plagues that will come generations after the life of the second beautiful one.

The parallels continue. The eleven sons of Jacob and their families travel the very same road into Egypt that Sarah and Abraham traveled in Gen 12.

If we stand just out of sight again on that road out of Canaan, we see all Sarah's seed travel into Egypt as if she herself walks this stretch again. She is no longer barren, and the beginnings of the promised multitudes like stars and sand go into Egypt. Can we see Sarah in them? Can we see in their hands or their hair or the shape of their faces the things that made Sarah beautiful? They too are beautiful ones brought into Egypt. We stand, and we listen to the sounds of Jacob, the brothers and their families talking moving traveling.

Years before, Abraham walked this road full of fear. His grandson Jacob is afraid too. Jacob has had roadside dreams before, and now he has another. God tells him not to be afraid. Are Sarah's descendants afraid? Do they know how dangerous Egypt was for Sarah—so dangerous that God sent plagues to rescue her? What plays in the minds of the mothers and the fathers as they lay to sleep beside that road, or wake in the early hours for another day of walking out of the land God promised and into the land that enslaved Sarah and that would someday enslave her seed?

Joseph's story is bigger than Sarah's. Big things happen, and there is great movement in each scene. Joseph is thrown into a deep pit—a horrible descent. He is brought up to a position of great power—an inconceivable climb. The brothers strip Joseph of what adorns him as the treasured son and Pharaoh clothes him as if Joseph is his firstborn. Joseph is carried into slavery away from his father in a caravan, but he rides out to meet him in a glorious chariot.

In Joseph's story, miles of land between Egypt and Canaan get covered over and over seemingly quickly. There is a feeling of expanse and largeness and movement. There is extreme famine and huge storehouses of grain. All the land experiences hunger and all the people come to Joseph for sustenance. Year after year comes and goes, and finally the entire land is sold back to Pharaoh under Joseph, and every person in all of Egypt sows the seeds Pharaoh owns on the land Pharaoh holds.

When Joseph brings the brothers and their families into Egypt, Pharaoh gives the entire region of Goshen to them as if there is so much land and space that Goshen large and plenty seems to be simply waiting for Joseph's family to populate. Joseph is fully aware of what God has done in his life. He proclaims that God sent him "to preserve life." His life and its effect is large, and he knows it and he proclaims it. Those dreams of his have come to pass, years of plenty and the years of famine. Eleven stars bow down before him, and the huge land is ready for Sarah's seed.

Sarah's story is very small compared to the expansiveness of Joseph's. Other than the one trip into and out of Egypt, Sarah's movement is limited to the travels of Abraham within the land of Canaan. Sarah moves among and within tents that move small distances within a small land.

But Sarah's story, not Joseph's, is the one with the greater magnitude. Sarah is the Linekeeper par excellence. She is the effective unprotected protector. The prophecy about the eleven stars comes to pass for Joseph in Egypt, but the prophecy about multitudes of stars like sand for Sarah and Abraham comes to pass for all times and in all places. Because of Joseph's protective action in Egypt, the entire Ancient Near East, the people, the land and even the seeds to plant the land come under Pharaoh. Because of Sarah's protective action in Egypt, the father of nations lives so that all people in all places for all times might come under God's protection, sustenance, and green new garden life.

The story of Joseph expansive shows how the story of Sarah small explodes. What seems tiny like a seed and hopeless like a barren woman bursts forth. It really does go well because of Sarah.

THINKING ABOUT SARAH'S LAUGHTER

There is nothing funny about being thrown away. There is nothing funny about betrayal—a deep wound inflicted at close range. There is nothing funny about finding yourself in a pit when all you wanted was a home, and there is something sickly laughable about a home barely recognizable.

As we begin to build our guess of why Sarah laughed, we must also wonder why God affirms her laughter when she denies it. "Yes, you did laugh." Past interpretation has jumped to the conclusion that Sarah laughed because she did not believe God's promise that day when he came to her tent to tell her she would have a son. Past interpretation has proven the assumption by figuring that when God said to her, "Yes, you did laugh," he was catching Sarah in some guilty, unfaithful lie.

If the story of the Bible is a story we read in order, that introduces us to God, perhaps it teaches us that what God intimately hears like no one else can hear is power God will use against us. Perhaps if past interpretation is true, God is pleased to catch Sarah in her lie. Gotcha.

But what if this is not so? What if God is not a God who would embarrass a hidden woman and show her a thing or two about how transparent and guilty she is?

Sarah's laughter sits between two very important events: when Abraham sells her to the first powerful man and when Abraham sells her to the second.

When Sarah laughs in her tent, and God hears and affirms it, Sarah does not yet know this second danger will happen to her. But maybe she feels it. Maybe her laughter has pain and hurt attached to it and maybe that pain and hurt is so pervasive in her life that it lives in a place that knows something horrible will happen again.

What if when God says to Sarah, "Yes, you did laugh," God is letting Sarah know that God knows what is going on inside her? What else might God know? What else might God understand? If God hears hidden laughter, perhaps God knows all the things in Sarah's life that came before that laughter. In affirming her laughter, perhaps God is acknowledging the importance of it and the importance of all the things that lead up to it. It is one thing for Abraham to relegate his barren wife to obscurity, but this is something Sarah's God refuses to do.

What if the God who hears unhearable things hears not only Sarah's laughter but also the cry inside it? What if God knows and sees what Abraham has done in the past to Sarah? What if he knows and sees what he will do again? And what if God affirms her laughter so that he can affirm the cry he hears in it too? Perhaps God simply wants Sarah to know that he hears her.

We look up from our Bibles. Does God affirm what God does not want us to deny?

Stick to your story, Sarah. I know your story. I was with you on the road, and I was with you in that harem. I heard your cry and I moved for you. I will hear you and I will move for you again. Yes, you did laugh. I hear it.

CHAPTER 5

Shall I Have . . . ?

Waking consciousness dawns and slowly overtakes deep sleep. Barrenness is an ugly surprise, a heart-falling realization, and a new sting in a new day. And now, there is emptiness on barrenness. There are no stirrings, no pain, no rhythm. Hope hurts but hopelessness hurts more. Barrenness backward and forward and now emptiness with the dawn of each day.

It is Sarah's turn to ask a question. God asked a hard question of the woman in the garden. Abraham asked Sarah, please lie. And now Sarah asks a new question.

"Shall I have . . . ?" Translations of this question have Sarah asking something like "shall I have pleasure?" But the Hebrew root of the word often translated "pleasure" is the same root for the name of the garden: "Eden."

A reader of Hebrew would see this connection—how the word Sarah uses in her question corresponds with the name of the garden. Unless we read Hebrew, we do not. It is essential that we see this, though. We must think about Eden because these stories are carefully crafted. There are other words that could have been used in Sarah's question, but the word of God gives us this one.

Why this word? How astute is Sarah's question? The desire for a child has deeper ramifications for a hopeful mother than for a hopeful father. Sarah has one less tier of security around her life

64

without a son. A widow without a son is vulnerable. At least Abraham has himself. And yet, there is nothing in her response to God's promise of a son to signal this consideration. Shall I have security? Shall I be provided for? No. Sarah asks, "Shall I have . . . Eden."

Shall she? How could she? The blessed thing is torn asunder. Sarah is far from the garden. Unity has given way to pain for both the man and the woman.

Heat of the day still and slow. Cool of the day wind in the trees. Trees of the garden. Oaks of Mamre. Wind in the trees in the heat of the day. The man is alone, and the woman is hidden. The woman is alone, and the man is hidden. Silent in the background. Heat of the day still and slow. Wind in the trees in the heat of the day. Where . . . Are . . . You . . . ?

BEFORE . . .

In the garden, before the matter of the tree, the man and the woman have gifts given to each meant to be used by and for both. In the garden, there is no hierarchy. Both the man and the woman share the high name and the high calling. They are God's image—male and female.

The woman is named help like the help of God, but this does not mean this high name is only for the woman; it is something humanity is to be for each other. God gives the law to the man before the woman is created. God tells him not to eat of the tree of the knowledge of good and evil. But this does not mean that the giving of the law is only for the man. The high name, help like the help of God, and the high calling, to be doers of the law, are for all humanity. It is only our perspective on this side of the curse that makes the high name something silly and hierarchal, as if the help of God is reduced to the subservience of a sidekick. And it is only our experience of the curse that makes the man presume he is made for some high place because the law was given to him.

The giving of the law in the garden does not depict a hierarchy. Instead, we see a progression of how humans relate to the law that begins with the man and is completed with the woman. The man receives the law. The woman interacts with it.

When God completes humanity with the creation of the woman, humanity begins to wrestle with what God has said, and human relationship with the law becomes deeper and more complex. We discussed above how in Ancient Near Eastern understanding the woman is associated with wisdom. This is why we see the woman under the tree with the serpent and why it is the woman who speaks to him about God's command. She interprets the law. Or as the ancient rabbis would say, she "builds a fence" around it. In other words, she takes God's law and considers ways to ensure human obedience to it. Not only must we not eat of the tree, but we really ought not touch it either. Thus, a "fence" built to stack the deck towards obedience.

The woman in the garden is like a rabbi. She knows just what God has said to humanity. God's word is hers. She uses "we" and the plural form of "you" when she tells the serpent what God has said. "We" may eat. "You" shall not eat, "you" shall not touch, "you" will die. Both the man and the woman are included. No part of humanity is marginal when it comes to knowing, considering, or obeying the law. The woman is the one who converses with the serpent, but the man is "with her." The prepositional phrase "with her" in Hebrew does not denote location, but togetherness—a joint participation. They are equal opposite sides.

The man and the woman are with each other in the high name God gives to all humanity. The man and the woman are with each other when it comes to what God says. They are physically in each other's presence, unified in a way that is hard, or maybe even impossible, for us conceptualize. All this is what is going on in the human relationship in the garden when what God says swirls in the air around them, green and new. The words that live on the page still today would sound completely different spoken to the ears of unified humanity. Rule together like my help. God's words fall on minds who do not immediately begin to grab, hide, and hoard. Something works seamlessly, and gifts given to each meant to be used by both kick in. The coach is still a coach.

AFTER . . .

If we are reading the story in order, the moment God comes to Sarah's tent then, is particularly striking.

The woman in the garden knows just what God has said. Sarah does not. There is no hint in the narrative that Abraham has told Sarah about the promises God has made to him. The man and the woman in the garden are together with each other, one flesh, something to cling to. Sarah and Abraham are not. Abraham has sold Sarah once and will soon sell her again to another man. The garden is fertile, and Sarah is barren. The garden is green, and Sarah is dust. The garden is lost, and Sarah is hidden.

There is a turning and flaming sword in each one of us . . .

If we think about Gen 18 as if it is a scene on a stage, and as if the placement of the characters and the scenery is meaningful, we begin to see. At first glance, the scene is familiar. It reminds us of the garden. There is a man and a woman under trees. But something has changed. The oaks of Mamre are different than the trees of the garden. There is something off. The tear looms as if it is superimposed on the background of the scenery, a great gash across the background of sky and trees and land. This is no garden.

After the flurry of hospitality, Abraham stands alone under the trees while the men eat what he and Sarah have prepared. The last time we have seen anyone eating under a tree was back in the garden when the man and the woman eat the fruit from the tree of the knowledge of good and evil together. Now in Gen 18, it is God who eats under a tree and the man is with him. Sarah is hidden.

Cover like nakedness. Hide like fear. Shame like a lie.

Under these trees God does not ask "where are you?" to the man like God did in the garden. Instead, he asks Abraham, "Where is your wife, Sarah?" When Abraham answers, he does not use Sarah's name and title of wife like God just has. He simply says, "Behold, in the tent." If we are reading the story in order, we might gasp. Though the men use Sarah's name, Abraham does not. The man and woman in the garden had a high name—help like the help of God. To Abraham, Sarah is nameless.

God tells Abraham that he will return the following year and that Sarah will have a son. This is the only time in the narrative where we see Sarah within earshot of a conversation between God and Abraham about God's promises. Under the first tree, the woman knows all about the things God talks about. Now under these trees, Sarah does not know. Up until now, what God has said to Abraham is not for her. And again, if we are reading in order, or watching this like a scene on a stage, our eyes squint, and we lean in closer. Could this really be?

What has happened to the height of the woman? The perfectly symmetrical opposite side hides in the tent. She is afraid when God hears her hidden laugh, and she lies. She is more like the man in the garden who hears God, fears, and hides than she is the woman of God's intention.

Sarah is far from Eden. She is nameless and barren. She is separated from the action, and she is separated from the knowledge of what God has said to Abraham all those times when God came to talk to him.

Like trees bending Sarah is old dust flying when God comes like a storm long ago. Where are you?

Where is the barren, nameless, hidden, separated woman? God wants to know.

Abraham answers the visitors. "There in the tent." Abraham knows just where she is today. Abraham, who on another day asked her please enter the palace of Pharaoh in Egypt—asked her please disappear into the shadows, to a place where he did not know where she was, or what she was experiencing. Abraham, who on another day soon will ask her please to do the same in the household of Abimelech. So, in the renewed stillness after the activity of hospitality the visitors ask Abraham, "Where is your wife, Sarah?"

How astute is God's question to Abraham? Where is Sarah, your wife? How deep and dark is it? What have you done? Where is the wife you have handed and will hand again into the hands of another man? Where is this woman who is not nameless? She is "Sarah, your wife." Is it at all possible that Abraham pauses and reckons a sting in God's inquiry? His answer is simple. To

Abraham, she is not "Sarah," and she is not "wife." She is "there in the tent." But the visitors name her twice. "Sarah, your wife."

Up to this moment, the narrative has also named Sarah twice. Sarah is "barren," and Sarah is "without children," as if barren and without children is everything she is. Up to this moment when God comes to her tent and changes things, perhaps "barren" and "without children" is all she thinks she is too. Maybe this is why they repeat her name and title twice. And maybe this is why they announce that she will have a son twice. "Behold! A son for Sarah!" (18:10). "For Sarah, a son!" (18:14).

Like wind suddenly shifting, the three men speak the reversal of "Sarai was barren; she had no child" (11:30) and "Now Sarai, Abram's wife had borne him no children" (16:1). She is "Sarah wife," and she is "for Sarah a son."

It matters what we call people.

SHALL I . . . ?

Shall there arise in Sarah springs of life in the place where there was dust? Shall the woman barren backwards and forwards be a part of something new? Could Sarah whose life lives out the destruction of the garden really be a part of something of repair and restoration and healing? What if Sarah's question speaks the hope and the promise of Eden?

The scene is filled with questions. Is there a tiny glimmer of hope in Sarah's? Could that barren woman hidden in the tent have any idea of what God is doing with her and for the world that she would ask about more than simple pleasure, and that her question would have something to do with Eden?

Even if Eden has nothing to do with what Sarah asks, it is enough to think of Sarah anticipating "pleasure." How does realization hit a woman standing alone in her empty tent? Surely there is a moment when Sarah understands what God is saying, when the words land in her mind. If pleasure really is all she anticipates, her question is practical. She and Abraham are old. The question is private. Not only is Sarah "barren," but "the way of woman has ceased with Sarah." The question is painful. What would it take for this old couple whose hope for a child died long ago? What would it take for a couple whose relationship must have been scarred by Sarah's time in Egypt to come together and to have "pleasure?" Would pleasure take a reigniting of something that had long ago burnt out or perhaps had never even existed in the first place? Pleasure might take an act of courage for the woman sold to Egypt to allow herself to be held in the hands of the one who sold her, held in the hands of the one who would someday soon sell her again.

What would it take for Abraham? Apparently, God anticipates some sort of challenge for the old man. We get a little hint of this when God responds to Sarah's question. It is one of the funniest moments in the story of Scripture. God knows that Sarah has questioned the whole idea of pleasure because of her age. She and God both know that the way of woman has ceased with her. But she has also questioned pleasure because of Abraham's age.

Now, to readers who are familiar with the precedent of the men of the ancient genealogies fathering children much further into old age than Abraham is at the moment of God's visit, Sarah's question is comical. We might chuckle right along with Sarah. But God's decision to leave the part about Abraham's age out when he repeats Sarah's question to him is downright hilarious. What does God know about Abraham that makes him give Sarah's question a little spin before it is repeated? Especially if Sarah is asking about pleasure.

But what if Sarah's question is about Eden?

We might hesitate to conclude that Sarah the person has any pious understanding of God's great plan to see his intention through. To produce a seed who would crush the head of the serpent, who would destroy the evil that arose after the matter of the tree, who would somehow restore the blessings of Eden to the world: unity in humanity, unity between humanity and the earth, and unity between humanity and God. But the word of God places the question on her lips sure as the word of God depicts the effective action of the Linekeepers to produce and to protect the seed. And I think that might be the point. Whether Sarah the person understands her part in God's plan or not, her words live on the page. Shall I have Eden?

WONDERFUL . . .

Now one of the things to consider as we wrestle with what Sarah meant by her question is God's question in response. If Sarah's question uses a word that is loaded with meaning, God's question does too. God asks, "Is anything too wonderful for the Lord?"

The word "wonderful,"[1] sometimes translated "difficult" or "hard" is a special word in Scripture. This "wonderful" is the kind of wonderful God will do for Sarah, but it is also the kind of "wonderful" God will continue to do for the children who will come from her. It is as if what God does for his people begins in the life of their mother.

In Exodus it describes how God stretches out his hand to perform wonders before Pharaoh in Egypt to free the Israelites out of slavery there.[2] Those wonders are for Pharaoh, so that he might see who God is. Later in Exodus the word describes the wonders[3] God will do for God's people, so that they might see who God is. In Joshua, God tells the people he will do wonders[4] among them and be present with them when he brings them into the promised land. The Psalms are full of this "wonderful" that describes not just a God who is majestic and holy in who God is but a God who is full of lovingkindness in what God does.

Sarah's question is hidden within her, within the dark folds of the tent, but God's question is bright and clear for all to hear.

---

1. The NRSV translates *pala* as "wonderful." Others translate it "difficult." However when we look at the other ways the word is used in the Torah and the one time it is used in Joshua, I think the NRSV translation "wonderful" gets closer to the point of the passage. "Difficult" is interesting too, though—I wonder if a nice translation would be "is anything too wonderful or too difficult for the Lord?"

2. Exod 3:20.

3. Exod 34:10.

4. Josh 3:5.

Is anything too miraculous, too freedom-giving for the one who does wonders and who works goodness? No. And this kind of wonderful is not just a wonderful that gives pleasure and sweetness and joy. It certainly is that. But it is more than that. This is the wonderful that gives freedom and green and newness and miracle in the place where there was captivity and dust.

God's question asks and remembers and jumps forward. It springs from God's mouth and swirls in the air and remembers the things God has done in the past for good and it jumps forward and changes the air around Sarah with something new right then at that moment in history. If we are silent in the background and watching, standing perhaps under the trees with the men or hidden somewhere also in the tent, we might feel it. We might even almost see this new thing that changes everything.

God's question remembers his great garden promise. God is about to plant a seed in the thorny ground with the birth of a baby to a barren woman. God is beginning the great cosmic work he promised to humanity as they were leaving the garden. God's question remembers what he did for Sarah, how he heard her cries and freed her. It remembers and it jumps forward. Just as God freed Sarah from Egypt and gave her fertility, God will free her children and plant them in a fertile land so Sarah's seed may grow to be a great people. God's question jumps forward even more, for God will free the hearts of all the people in all the world in all times and places because of the seed that would come from the great people who would come from Sarah.

God's question, "Is there anything too wonderful for the Lord?" then, is about that seed. It remembers the garden promise and looks ahead to that promise coming to pass. It promises a seed for Sarah—a child. But it also promises a seed from Sarah—a people. And from that people would come the promised seed—the Savior. That promised Savior seed would come to free and heal and restore and forgive. That Savior seed will bring the world not backwards to a garden of goodness and unity but forward to a world redeemed—a garden grown to be a city where the city of God is the garden spread everywhere. Nothing is too hard or wonderful for God.

If God's question is about the seed, why shouldn't Sarah's question be about the garden? If God's question harkens us to wonderful things of freedom and newness and green, why shouldn't Sarah's?

God will take away barren and give Sarah a baby. God will take away hidden and give her laughing. God will take away the un-Edenlike things in her life and replace them with something new. Because of the great freedom and life and green giving thing that will come from the seed God is about to grow for Sarah, God will work good with un-Edenlike things in all times and places. For Sarah, a son. Shall Sarah have Eden? Shall we?

SARAH'S NAME

What seems to be going on here? What does it mean that Abraham does not use Sarah's name or her title as wife? If we ground Sarah's story in the rest of the story of Scripture by going back to the garden, we see an important key to understanding Abraham's unnaming of Sarah. We have already discussed how the man and the woman in the garden share the high name and the high calling together as one flesh and how in the story of Sarah it is lost. But there is something else we must see.

Before God completes humanity with the creation of the woman, God brings the animals to the man so that the man can name them. When the man names the animals, the text uses a standard Hebrew phrase that uses both the word "call" and the word "name." This pattern is often translated "called the name." It is a common phrase used when someone with authority names someone or something with lesser authority, like when a parent names a child. So, when the man calls the name of the animals it signifies humanity's rule over the animals of the earth.[5] This is something God sanctions by bringing the animals to the man so that he can establish his rule over them by naming them.

---

5. Trible, *God and the Rhetoric of Sexuality*, 99.

However, when God brings the woman to the man, and the man calls her "woman," the man does not use the naming formula "called the name." Instead, the man simply "calls" her "woman." "The noun 'name' is strikingly absent from the poetry. In 'calling' the woman, the man is not establishing power over her but rejoicing in their mutuality."[6]

After the curse, as humanity is leaving the Garden, the man renames the woman "Eve." When he does this, the Hebrew text repeats the naming formula "called the name" that the man used when he was naming the animals. In "calling the name" of Eve, the man confirms her lowered status.[7] She is no longer one to exclaim unity over, she is instead one to declare rule over. Once God's intended unity is destroyed, God's words of consequence begin to unfold. It is as if in "calling the name" of Eve, the man is staking a claim on his newfound dominion over her.

However, there is a sharp contrast here in the text that we must not miss. God brought the animals to the man so that he could name them in a way that declared rule over them. God brought the woman to the man so that he could name her in a way that declared mutuality in humanity. But God never brings the woman to the man for him to rename her. The text simply tells us that the man "called her the name Eve." God does not participate in the renaming of the woman that declares the rule of the man over her.

We look up from our Bibles, and we think about how this time, God is the one silent and in the background. Here too is a deep, hard question. Why does God allow the effects of the curse? Wouldn't there be some other way? Haven't we just pondered the fact that God is a God who does not stand back blithely? God sees and hears and helps Sarah. Why does God allow the man to name the woman a name that declares his rule over her? Where is God? We have already discussed how the story shows us that God is not complicit with the effects of the curse, so why does God stand silent and allow the man to declare rule, and then live rule, over the woman?

---

6. Trible, *God and the Rhetoric of Sexuality*, 100.

7. Trible, *God and the Rhetoric of Sexuality*, 132–34.

Why is Abraham allowed to follow suit with all the men from the first one in the garden through Cain and Lamech and Noah, and why must Sarah fall in line with all their unnamed and silent wives? Like a woman on a dusty road into a land of slavery humanity walks on. God, silent in the background, lets it happen. God doesn't cry foul, rush in, and sweep humanity back up into the garden to start over. Sarah and Abraham do not seem to have a homesick pull there anyway.

We stand silent too. What is this light and angle and color? What is God's heart here? We pause because to fail to pause risks filling in the text with the quick interpretation that what we see is what we get: a God complicit in the effects of the curse, who spoke consequences he agrees with, who is just waiting in the background for the opportunity to consign the woman to obscurity.

The history of interpretation really can make it seem that way, that the effects of the curse are things God agrees with. The unity of the garden is a tiny little fleeting moment that gets consumed by the history of the torn apart thing that introduced hierarchy. And hierarchy is everywhere. Women have been nameless and consigned to the background for all history. If we are not careful, we find our thinking lives in the pit humanity has created for itself. Men are at the forefront of the narrative, and that is where God would have them since that is what is in the Bible.

Instead, we must wrestle with the text to see. What is God's heart here? It is there if we look with fresh eyes to see it. Mysteriously, God allows the curse to stand, but with the help of humanity, God works against it. God's heart is hidden and in the background with the woman.

We go back to the story like it is a scene on a stage. Sarah is hidden and God asks where she is. I think there is a sting in that question. "Where is Sarah, your wife?" Abraham dares to respond. "There in the tent." He does not seem to recognize the sting.

Abraham might not use the new name God gave Sarah. He might even call her "sister" to yet another powerful man soon after this. But God comes to Sarah's tent that day long ago and contradicts Abraham. The three men repeat Sarah's name and her status of wife so much that it is comical. It is as if the visitors are there to remind or even command Abraham to recognize who Sarah is.

Not only does God give Sarah this new name, but God names her a name that includes her in the great Eden thing God is doing. God told Abraham in Gen 12 that God will make Abraham's name great. In Gen 17, God gives Sarah a great name too. Now at this moment at Sarah's tent, God insists on it.

To God they are more than people living in the wake of the destruction of the garden, they are "Abraham, exalted father" and "Sarah, mother of nations." Somehow in some miraculous green freedom giving way they will be a blessing to all the families of the earth.

For Sarah, a son. For Sarah, Eden—blessing like sand and stars too many to count.

SARAH INCLUDED . . .

If Sarah is essential to the fulfillment of the promises God makes to Abraham, why doesn't God call Sarah at the same time he calls Abraham? Sarah is not present in that moment of Gen 12 when God comes to Abraham. If she is there, she is silent and in the background.

In Gen 15, God appears to Abraham and specifically tells him that he will have a son "from his own body." It is hard to imagine that Sarah is there for this meeting either, because so much happens and there is no mention of her. The sense of the story is that what goes down is a private interaction between God and Abraham. God tells Abraham to number the stars if he can. He assures Abraham of his fidelity with the strange rite of the animals and the fire pot and the birds of prey. Abraham falls into a deep and terrified sleep where God reveals to him the certainty of the Egyptian slavery of the people God has just promised him.

Immediately after the Gen 15 meeting between God and Abraham, Sarah gives Hagar to Abraham in the hopes that perhaps the union will produce a child. The text tells us just why Sarah does this. She hopes that she will be "built up" by using Hagar. She hopes that Hagar will produce a child Sarah can claim as her own. Would Sarah have done this if she had known God's promise, and that it included her? We do not know. What we do know is that Abraham complies. What else can his compliance mean than to Abraham, Sarah has nothing to do with God's promise? Why share the wonderful news with her?

In Gen 17, God comes to Abraham again and tells him that the promised son will come from Sarah. Abraham laughs and asks if perhaps God might divert the plan a little. Abraham would prefer that Hagar, not Sarah, be the mother of those promised nations. If there is any question in our minds about how Abraham feels about Sarah's inclusion in the promises God has made to him, this interaction clears them up. But the interaction between God and Sarah in Gen 18 clears a few things up too. In Gen 18 we see that regardless of how Abraham feels about her, Sarah is essential to God.

In Gen 18, God comes for Sarah. But God has some questions for Abraham. The questions are as deep and dark as the question God asks the woman in the garden. But this time the deep, dark questions are for the man. Perhaps God is indignant that Abraham has not shared with Sarah the "wonderful" information God has shared with him. How could this woman who is key to the promises made to Abraham be hidden and nameless? "Why did Sarah laugh" at what should have come as no surprise to her? God's first question to Abraham should have shamed him. "Where is Sarah, your wife?" This question ought to mortify him. "Why did Sarah laugh?" How could Abraham have kept this wonderful information from Sarah? How could Abraham not call her "Sarah, wife" when God calls her "Sarah, wife"?

God needs to ask the question of Abraham as much as God needs to ask the man where he is in the garden. The question is for the man, not for the God. And if the man will take no action to include her, the God will.

Here, again, we go back to the garden to have a look. It is significant that the narrative depicts God speaking separately to the man and to the woman after the matter of the tree. When God cast humanity out of the garden, Gen 3:24 tells us that God "drove out the man." There is no mention of the woman, but we know that she is with him, silent and in the background, because the narrative picks up and includes her later in the story.

If we are reading the story in order, we see that the same sort of thing happens with Abraham and Sarah. God comes to Abraham to tell him to go into the promised land. There is no mention of Sarah until the narrative tells us that Abraham takes her along. The man alone is cast out of the garden, and Abraham alone is beckoned into the promised land.

There is a mysterious pattern here. God states the effects of the curse and God allows the effects of the curse, even going so far as to operate within it by addressing the man and the woman separately. God throws the man alone out of the garden, and God calls the man alone into the promised land. The pattern continues when God comes to Abraham alone in Gen 12, 15, and 17. But the pattern is broken in Gen 18.

When God comes to Sarah in Gen 18, it is an example of God working against the curse. Or perhaps we could say this: God operates within the effects of the curse by coming and speaking to Abraham alone. But when God comes to Sarah, God is not simply working against or contradicting the effects of the curse. God is doing something entirely new. Including Sarah is not going backwards to remember the old, lost unity of the garden and working against the corrupted state of things. Including Sarah ushers in the new thing God is doing. This new thing is so new that it does not need to harken back to the old. It is new growth and fresh green that will surpass the old good. It will grow something new out of what is barren and lost.

Shall Sarah have Eden? Yes. But Sarah will have more than Eden. If we read carefully, we find that there is not a theme in the Bible that returns humanity to Eden. Instead, the story uses images of a garden, like the fertile promised land and the Temple, to move the story forward from the garden. The forward motion and hope is indeed a garden, but it is not the old garden humanity left. The story propels forward to a new garden, which becomes a city with walls and open gates where all peoples from all times and places can enter.

Shall Sarah have Eden? If by Eden we mean that her seed grows to become nations and peoples from all times and places, then yes. Something new. Shall Sarah have Eden? Shall we? Yes. For like sand and stars, God has created redemption for humanity everywhere.

SARAH'S COVENANT CONFIRMATION

There is more to Sarah's inclusion in the great Eden thing God is doing than God simply coming to her and telling her that she will have a son and making sure she knows she is a part of things. Genesis 18 is Sarah's covenant confirmation ceremony.

In the garden after the curse, God interacts with the man and the woman separately. We see the same sort of thing when God comes to Abraham for his covenant confirmation in Gen 17 and then to Sarah for hers in Gen 18. Why this is the dynamic the narrative of the Bible depicts, I do not know, but it is essential that we see it. If we do not, we can fall into old, tired thinking that assumes that God only came to Abraham and that the covenant God enacted with him included Sarah only when she tagged along with him. But Sarah is essential to the covenant. She must be included, and God comes to her in Gen 18 to see to it that she is.

If we are reading the story in order, and if we have broken away from old, tired thinking, we are waiting to see how and when Sarah will be included. If we are reading this way, we see readily that Gen 17 and 18 go together. The two interactions echo each other. They are different in some ways of course, but they are clearly stitched together in the narrative and should be read together.

Of course, Gen 17 is not the first time God speaks with Abraham. God calls him in Gen 12 to leave his country and his family and to go to the land God would show him. In Gen 15, God comes to Abraham again to give him what I like to think of as the covenant of knowing.

Genesis 15 is famous for Abraham believing God's promise and God crediting that belief to him as if he is righteous for it. But Abraham has a question that follows the promise that is a bit less famous but is quite important. Abraham asks God how he can be sure that God will do what God has promised. God responds by enacting the covenant of knowing ceremony with Abraham. This strange ceremony in which the smoking fire pot moves between the cut-open animals shows Abraham that the promise God has just made to him rests fully on God's action. What God has just enacted for Abraham is akin to an Ancient Near Eastern oath that swears that the bonds of the covenant depend on the one who has made it. So, in enacting this covenant of knowing in Gen 15, God is taking full responsibility to see the promise of the covenant through. It is that declaration of responsibility for the whole thing that should assure Abraham of what he is looking for, a way to know that what God is promising will come to pass.

It is years later though, after Abraham and Sarah have conspired to have a son with Hagar, and after that son has grown to be thirteen years old when God comes to Abraham again in Gen 17. The visit is different this time. This time, Abraham must do something. Even though God made it clear in Gen 15 that the thing God is doing will happen because of God's determination that it will happen, in Gen 17, God requires Abraham to sign on to the whole deal. If Gen 15 is Abraham's covenant of knowing that God will do what God has said ceremony, Gen 17 is Abraham's covenant confirmation, joining-in ceremony.

Genesis 17 is the first time in all the interactions between God and Abraham that God calls Abraham a father. God promises Abraham great fertility and says that Abraham will be exceedingly numerous and the father of multitudes of nations. God repeats it again—Abraham will be full of fruit, nations, and kings will come from Abraham's "seed."

CIRCUMCISION AND COVENANTS

In the midst of all of this talk of fertility, God tells Abraham that he must be circumcised and that all of the men associated with Abraham must be circumcised too. Circumcision is the mark of Abraham's covenant confirmation joining-in ceremony.

Now, circumcision is a complex concept in the story of Scripture. At its simplest, circumcision was a fertility rite that was not uncommon in ancient times and was not just a thing that was practiced in Judaism. However, when God tells Abraham to circumcise his household, circumcision takes on a whole new spin.

Circumcision becomes the essential mark of all male Jews, and any male who is connected to a Jewish household. It becomes a mark of belonging. But more than a rite of fertility, more even than a mark of belonging, Jewish circumcision is a sign of commitment. Like their Ancient Near Eastern neighbors, Jews saw circumcision as an opening of the fertility of a man, essentially cutting away what could hinder the spreading of his seed. But the Jews especially saw circumcision as an outward sign of commitment to God—essentially cutting away in the heart what could hinder complete commitment to God and God's work in the world (Deut 10:16).

OPENED . . .

In order for Abraham to be a part of what God is doing, God requires Abraham to submit to this rite. Abraham must be opened and committed and ready to be God's partner. And, more than that, anyone who comes from Abraham who wants to have anything to do with what God is doing must do the same thing. Open and fertile by circumcision to have children, open and fertile of heart to do what God is calling those associated with Abraham to do.

When God comes to Abraham in Gen 15 and moves between the cut animals, God is saying that the whole deal of what God is doing, God's great plan, depends on God. This thing of redemption, of Eden, of goodness in the world, would happen because of

God, whether or not Abraham signs on. But God wants Abraham to sign on. It seems God loves the unity of the garden so much that even though God's great plan hangs on God's determination, God invites humanity to be a part of it all too. Open, fertile, committed, ready.

This third time God comes to Abraham in Gen 17 is different for another reason too. Before, God has told Abraham of descendants, but this time God tells him that those descendants will come from Sarah. Why God waits till the third interchange with Abraham to tell him that it is Sarah who will be the mother of nations we do not know. What we do know is that when Abraham is told of Sarah's involvement in those great promises, Abraham falls on his face and laughs. He questions God. Abraham's question provides an alternative; perhaps Ishmael should be the son of the promise.

Now, Gen 18 comes right after Gen 17. It seems obvious and even silly to say but it is important that we see this, for it is no coincidence. The story must be read in order. Abraham's laughter and question in Gen 17 is stitched together to Sarah's laughter and question that follows in Gen 18. By echoing each other, the narrative gives us a hint that the two incidents should be understood together.

God comes to Abraham, changes his name, and tells him he will be a father. God comes to Sarah, uses her changed name, and announces she will have a son. Abraham laughs and asks a question about being old, and Sarah laughs and asks a question about being old. God confirms by repetition to Abraham that it is indeed Sarah who will have the son who will fulfill the promises God has made to him. God confirms by repetition to Sarah that she will indeed have a son. Abraham obeys God in Gen 17 with the rite of circumcision. He is physically opened. His seed will not be hindered. Sarah receives God's promise at the doorway of her tent. She hears that her seed will not be hindered, that her womb will be opened.

Sarah's question in Gen 18 is more complex than Abraham's in Gen 17. It is a wonderful question that has to do with pleasure, or maybe even Eden. She laughs her question, just like Abraham laughs his. Her concern is the same as Abraham's. They are old. How can this be? But, unlike Abraham's, Sarah's laughter and question provide no alternative. Why would she do that? This plan sounds wonderful. Why should she fall on her face? Perhaps instead she lifted her head and tuned her ears. If Abraham's laughter denies Sarah's involvement, Sarah's laughter receives it.

In Gen 17, Yahweh appears to Abraham to see about Abraham's heart toward his whole plan—to confirm that it is open and ready for what God is planning to do with Abraham. In Gen 18, Yahweh comes to do the same thing with Sarah. The moment between God and Sarah in Gen 18 catches Sarah up on all the meetings Sarah was not a part of. Genesis 18 is Sarah's covenant confirmation joining-in ceremony.

The Eden thing God is doing in the world has to do with the land and the people who will be born on the land. For God to begin this Eden thing, there must be some sort of unity between the Landholders and the Linekeepers. Sarah must be in on the plan. When God comes to Sarah that day to tell her she would have a son the very next year at that time, that day is Sarah's opportunity to sign on—to be opened, committed, and ready. Just as God required Abraham to be circumcised as a physical sign of belonging and as a heart sign of commitment, God seeks the same openness and commitment from Sarah. The signs are a bit more subtle than Abraham's encounters with God, but they are there. We must listen carefully to find them, as if we too must overhear what is essential.

Has she listened carefully? The verdict on the head of the serpent is the omen in the hands of the woman. Two seeds. Each will strike but one will crush. How strange that the woman in the garden must overhear it. The one who wrestles with the word from God is the one who must now overhear it. What else must she overhear? This ruled-overness will spill out and over into all history and the woman's hearing is overhearing. But look again. Yahweh moves among the women.

TENTS AND COVENANTS

If the people interpreting the Bible for all these years had approached the text in a way that was as interested in women as it is in men, this sort of thing would have been obvious. It is there.

Here is another place we must remember that the interpretation of the text is a different thing than the text itself. Interpretation has focused on the stories of the men. But when we look with fresh eyes, we see that there is much to find about women. Certainly, the word of God itself lives in a place that is affected by the curse. It simply focuses more on men than it does on women. However, the text can and does reflect the heart of the God, who does not agree with and is working against the curse. The text can and does advocate for women and weave their stories into a background in which they are essential.

Not everyone agrees with this. Some scholars believe that the text of the Bible is so enmeshed in the curse of hierarchy and patriarchy that it cannot be redeemed. This approach focuses largely, if not exclusively on the human authorship of the Bible. And of course, we cannot deny that it is quite obvious that it was written by human men in a man's world. Indeed, we short-circuit the possibility of our good understanding if we fail to recognize the human fingerprints all over it.

But on the other hand, the Bible is different than anything else that has ever been written. Even though the human fingerprints can make it terribly ugly in places, it is also somehow mysteriously the word of God. This is not easy to understand or explain, but we have to keep it in mind as we wrestle with the text. Though men are at the forefront of the narrative, all humanity is important to the story, and all people are key in the heart of God. If for all these years we had been looking for this sort of thing, we would have found it. It is just not as easy to see, and it has not really been looked for. Our Bible studies and church sermons talk about Abraham's covenant. We do not talk about Sarah's. But it is there. Sarah's covenant with God had to happen for Abraham and Sarah to be involved in the Eden thing God was beginning.

Abraham's covenant confirmation happened under the stars and is marked by circumcision. Sarah's covenant confirmation happened at the opening of her tent, and it is marked by her laughter. It is significant that this happened at the opening of a tent. We will discuss why. Next, we will think about how the narrative uses images and words having to do with "opening," "Eden/pleasure," and "laughter" to depict what happened the day God appeared to Sarah.

TENT SETTING

At the beginning of the scene in Gen 18, Sarah is inside the tent. Now, tents are important in the Hebrew Scriptures. People live in tents from the beginning of life outside the garden. They are good places that God uses to protect and bless people. (Interestingly, it is a brick tower that spells trouble early in the story of the Bible.) Noah, Abraham, Isaac, Jacob, and the twelve tribes live in tents. They move with them as they travel, so in a sense, the place of home is a constant in the lives of these tent-dwelling wanderers. When God assures the people of God's protection, it is often in connection to God's presence among their tents. When God tells the people that he would dwell among them, it is in a tent. Moses called that tent where God would dwell a tabernacle, but "tent" and "tabernacle" are the same word in Hebrew and in the Greek Septuagint. It is also the word for the Tabernacle of the Temple in Jerusalem.

Sarah stands at her tent and meets with God. She is the first of generations of her children to come who would do such a thing. She is like Moses standing at the door of the tent of meeting. Moses returned from those meetings to offer the people the covenant. God gave them the law through Moses, a covenant so that they would be God's people. Sarah is like the high priests who would come from her seed generations from now and for generations to come. They too would stand at the entrance of a tent and contend with God. The covenant that gave them the law also gave them a way to come to the entrance of the tabernacle to receive forgiveness. All of these things begin at the door of Sarah's tent for generations after Sarah. All of these things begin with the moment Sarah stood there and became a part of the covenant.

Sarah is the first. All these things are within her waiting to be born: Moses, the priesthood, the times when her children would meet with God in the tabernacle of the Temple, all the times and all the places people would meet with God. These are the things ready to spring forth from the opening of the very first tent where God and Sarah talked to each other.

The opening of Sarah's tent points ahead to all the times to come when God will hear Sarah's children, and all the times to come when God will include Sarah's children. It is a covenant moment that points ahead to all the children who would come from Sarah in all the places of protection and comfort and in all the places of desolation and destruction.

Holy and strange. The air shifts and carries this new name did she hear it where are you? Just to the very close opening of her tent on the dusty ground in the heat of the day close as a breath . . . or a gasp in. God appears.

OPENINGS, LAUGHTER, AND PLEASURE

On this day, in the beginning of the story of all the children who would come from Sarah, she is inside the tent. It is the heat of the day, and Abraham is sitting outside the opening of the tent. The scene feels quiet and still and even heavy. This is the time of the day when things slow down. The work of the morning has ceased and the preparations for the evening have not yet begun. It is hot, time to be quiet. We do not know how long Abraham has been sitting or how long Sarah has been inside. It feels settled. It feels settled because of the sudden unsettled action that breaks the silence of the scene.

The Lord appears. Abraham slowly lifts his eyes. He looks, beholds, sees. The slow progression of recognition bursts into furious action. Abraham runs to the visitors, rushes back to the tent, runs to the herd and hurries to prepare the meal. Sarah is hurrying too, preparing, kneading, baking.

The action slows. Abraham places the meal before the visitors and stands back respectfully. Sarah is in the tent. Her hurrying is done. Still. Stillness. Abraham stands in the open, and Sarah moves hidden. Is she already standing at the opening of the tent or does the sound of this new name draw her there? We do not know, the text does not tell us, but at some point in the scene, Sarah moves to the opening of the tent.

Tents do not have solid doors. We must picture her moving to the opening, then standing there hidden in the folds of the entrance. It is from this hidden place among the opening folds of the tent that Sarah hears about another opening.

A reader of Hebrew would see this clearly. It might even make her laugh. The Hebrew word for opening or doorway that is used for the opening of a tent and the doorway of the tabernacle is the same word for the opening of a womb. Sarah moves to the opening of the tent to hear about the opening of her womb. The God who opens and closes wombs will open her closed one.

We hold the picture of Sarah at the opening of her tent—light, angle, color. We ponder Sarah's movement to the tent opening, her laughter, and the question she asks about pleasure or maybe even Eden. Remember, Gen 18 comes after Gen 17. We combine the images of openings, laughter, and pleasure and remember that they follow Abraham's circumcision. If we think of these images alongside circumcision, we must consider that they too are ideas and images that have to do with the opening of the fertility of a person.

Sarah moves to the opening folds of the tent to hear that her womb will be opened. Something has to change in a barren, dry body in order for it to be able to sustain life. Just as Sarah moves to the opening of tent to hear the wonderful news, moisture will move through her body to its opening folds. She is no longer like dust. Inside her will come alive and open like flowers. Her laugh bursts forth from a hidden place within the folds of the tent like moisture and fertility will burst forth new from the hidden folds of her body. Her green garden question wonders how all this could be. All these images swirl together for us to ponder the reality of the miraculous thing that is going on inside Sarah.

Open ready alive free new included green home soft stars wind blooming warmth opening bursting laughing pleasure watering Eden.

The story of Sarah is not a simple story. There is no bitter old lady who laughs at God because she does not believe what God promises. Her story is about what happens when something dead is enlivened to be ready to sustain life.

God's garden promise for the woman swirls in the air around Sarah's tent. God remembers the hope God spoke to the woman in the garden because God will not forget. Our first look at Sarah out on the road into Egypt makes us wonder if maybe God has forgotten. If there is any woman who endures the pain of childbearing it is a barren woman. But God appears. A million things of sadness combine with thousands of years of newness, and Sarah's laugh means many things. It means that Sarah remembers all of the bad things that have happened, and when God affirms her laugh it means God remembers too. It means that something new will burst forth from Sarah. It is not enough for God to contradict the effects of the curse in Sarah's life and in the lives of the ones who will come from her. God is doing something entirely new, as new as new life from dust.

Here is a small remembrance of the lost unity of the garden—the man and the woman both experience something foundational that initiates them into the work God will allow humanity to participate in. Abraham and Sarah both experience covenant confirmation moments. But Sarah's ceremony is not just a sort of circumcision, as if the experience of the woman must be merely an echo of the experience of the man. Sarah's ceremony is distinct. It takes an independent turn from Abraham's and adds an aspect of intimacy that we do not see in Abraham's circumcision ceremony. For Abraham, the text tells us that he obeyed and circumcised his household. The text does not tell us what went down between God and Abraham, so we do not know. However, the text does tell us about what happened between God and Sarah.

Sarah laughs when she hears God's promise. Unlike Abraham's face-falling guffaw, her laughter is hidden and silent deep within her, yet God hears it. Sarah's laughter shows us something foundational. It is not easily defined, so we mustn't call it one thing, wipe our hands, and move along as if we understand the moment and as if it is not meant to be held and turned—light, angle, color. It means something that God hears what is hidden, and more than that, it means something that God makes sure Sarah knows that she has been heard. What if God asks the question, "Why did Sarah laugh?" simply in order that Sarah might know that God actually heard her? The text does not tell us, so we do not know. But that day signals the second time in the story God hears Sarah. God hears. This is not lost on Sarah, so it should not be lost on us.

Sarah's ceremony is also distinct from Abraham's because it is less exclusive. Circumcision became a rite that distinguished Jewish males over Jewish females and non-Jews. Later in the history of the story of God's people it becomes something that separates and excludes. However, if laughter is the mark of Sarah's inclusion in the covenant, her laughter points ahead to a time when the desire to be included is the only barrier to entry to the green garden goodness of inclusion in the people of God. Interestingly, this is exemplified in the story of the Bible through women. We see women like Ruth and Rahab who are outsiders to the covenant God made with the Jews, yet they are included simply because of their desire to be included—as if they heard and wanted to laugh along with Sarah.

We look up from our Bibles and we think of the generations of Sarah . . . Abraham, Isaac, Jacob . . . from their beginning, with Sarah at the opening of the tent to the time of Jesus' Jerusalem, and we wonder. What does the promise of a seed who will crush the head of the serpent mean to a people whose necks have spent more time under the boots of Assyria, Babylon, Persia, Greece, Rome, than they have spent holding their own heads high? What does Sarah's new name mean to a people whose name has been taken from them over and over? Did the promise of something new startle Sarah's children into laughter and questions too? How can this be? How can what is barren and lost be redeemed? How can a people who have been relegated to obscurity and dispossessed of their land somehow imagine that God has a garden for them?

It is not hard to imagine that the children who come from Sarah, both men and women, might relate more closely with her experience than with Abraham's. To a nation whose history is dominated by domination, the children of Sarah might see themselves in the tent with Sarah, not in the place where the powerful come from battles with kings to talk with gods. They might see themselves hidden and unheard, cast aside and always at risk of being sold into the hands of the powerful instead of being powerful themselves.[8]

There is solace at the opening of Sarah's tent for men and for women. If we are reading the story in order, and if we are just learning about God, the place of the entrance of the tent where God appeared to Sarah establishes again that God is a god who appears and approaches and who hears the unhearable and who gives wonderful things in a place where wonderful things are lost. God opens things even when it seems things are hopelessly closed.

There is intimacy at the opening of Sarah's tent for men and for women. God is doing a great Eden thing in the world to fix the broken unity that happened there. This is a cosmic thing that involves all the families of the earth, all the nations in all the times and places. But this is also a thing that God does for each of us. God sees and hears and knows.

Like being jolted out of sleep, not slowly awakened. Realization bursts forth like a laugh as if already the sadness that came before in sleepy stillness wakes into plain old sweet happiness. Something hidden inside moves silent. Folds bloom enlivened.

---

8. This is an idea that Tikva Friemer-Kensky repeats often in her analysis of the women of the Hebrew Scriptures. It is one of the most compelling things I have ever heard about how the Bible depicts women.

CHAPTER 6

"God Has Made Laughter for Me and Everyone Who Hears Will Laugh with Me . . ."

LAUGHTER IN THE STORY of Genesis is Sarah's. It is at her expense, and it is hers to laugh. The key to Sarah's laughter is that God hears it. "Yes, you did laugh." God affirms her laughter, and when Isaac is born Sarah attributes laughter to God and says it is something come from God, as if God is laughing too.

Even the name of her promised baby remembers laughter. Isaac means "He Laughs." Every time Sarah would call her little boy, she might remember her laughter and how God heard it when God appeared at her tent that day. But with a slight turn of the prism the idea of laughing becomes more complex. This laughter Sarah says comes from God becomes laughter that others will laugh with her because of her, as if laughter is a gift.

Right after she says this about the laughter God has given her, the narrative skips to the feast Abraham throws when Isaac is weaned. Sarah sees Ishmael doing something with Isaac. The "something" is the same word in Hebrew for "laugh." But it is challenging to translate. Is Ishmael joking with Isaac? Is he teasing or laughing at him? Since Isaac means "he laughs," you could also read it to say that Sarah saw Ishmael not laughing but "Isaacing." Is

Ishmael trying to be like Isaac? Perhaps he realizes his subordinate role to this little brother, and he is trying somehow to usurp Isaac's position. That sort of thing happens quite a bit in Genesis.

If we take a stab at what is going on at the feast, we might figure that this is indeed Sarah's concern and the reason she wants to get rid of Ishmael. She says it quite plainly. When she sees Ishmael doing whatever he is doing with Isaac, she declares that Ishmael must not "inherit" with Isaac. She does not want Ishmael to have anything that might infringe upon what might be Isaac's. Both Abraham and God have to agree with Sarah. Sarah has heard God's talk. God has also spoken plainly. Isaac is the child of the promise, not Ishmael. "For it is through Isaac that offspring shall be named for you." God has said it, and Sarah will see it through. There is a line to keep.

It seems Sarah's problem is solved. But things are not so simple. God has also made it quite plain that he would have great concern for Ishmael. Ishmael means "God Hears." When Hagar calls her son's name it might remind her of God's concern. Whenever Ishmael speaks his own name, he repeats again the promise God made to his mother concerning him.

Why then does God tell Abraham to listen to Sarah's voice and to cast him out of the family? Why is Abraham's son and his mother sent out to the desert with little more than a day's provisions? Hagar's name means "Wanderer."

Motherless no past. Out. No line to hold you. Barren. Unchosen. Your name is slave . . . or childless . . . or beautiful . . . or wanderer. It matters what we call people.

If we are reading the story in order, we are also wondering what Sarah's mysterious statement means. Who is she talking about? Who will hear the laughter God has given to Sarah and laugh along with her? Surely her statement means more than how it is commonly read, that people will laugh with and at her because it is funny that someone so old would have a baby. There is not much in the text to signal this anyway. There does not seem to be any sort of community that surrounds Abraham and Sarah. There is no circle of women who come around Sarah at the birth of her son. There is the feast Abraham throws when Isaac is weaned, but no guests are identified.

Who will laugh with Sarah?

Since Sarah's exclamation and her casting out of Hagar and Ishmael happen right next to each other in the narrative we must consider their connection. After all, Ishmael's name and his action at the feast encompass Sarah's statement about who will be included in her laughter. He is doing exactly what she says will happen. "God Hears" laughs with "He Laughs." The one who is named for hearing is laughing with Isaac, the laughter God gave to Sarah. Is Ishmael the one who hears? For Sarah's statement is a pun not only on the name of the son named for laughing, "He Laughs," but also on the son named for hearing, "God Hears."

Anyone who hears will laugh with me . . .

Now these are strange things to think about because the Genesis story is all about who is in and who is out—who is included in the covenant God made with Abraham and Sarah and who is not. Not only that, but it is clear Hagar and Ishmael are out. Abraham specifically asks if Ishmael might be the child of God's promise, and God specifically replies, "No." God comes to Sarah's tent to affirm that Sarah is the mother of the promise. The other woman is excluded. At this point in the story the covenant is really only about the people who would descend from Abraham and Sarah. God is the God of Abraham, Isaac, and Jacob. At this point it seems that the only people who might laugh with Sarah are the people who are "in" that line.

But the thing Sarah says when the promised, included child is born says something about the excluded child—the one God allowed Abraham to send away. The story is doing something here that we must not miss if we are to begin to understand Sarah's laughter. Even though Sarah casts Ishmael out, Sarah's statement that precedes her action seems to include him. It seems Ishmael is part of "everyone who hears" and therefore part of those who will laugh along with Sarah. This does not mean that the line Sarah keeps is changing to include Ishmael. God has made things clear. "For it is through Isaac that offspring shall be named for you."

However, the laughter Sarah laughs signifies something very important about the purpose of the line Sarah keeps.

THE LINE OF THE COVENANT AND ITS PURPOSE

At the very beginning of the covenant, God chose one family, Abraham and Sarah, to begin the line of people God would eventually use to bless all the families of the earth. At its beginning, however, the line was so limited to this particular family that we really can say that the book of Genesis is a book about who is "in" and who is "out." Only Abraham and Sarah's family is "in." Even more than that, only certain people within Abraham and Sarah's family are "in."

There is no evidence in the text that God has any preference or particular love for those he chooses. From what we can see, God simply chooses. God chose Seth over Cain and Abel. Of Noah's sons, God chose Shem. Abraham had other sons from other women, but God chose Isaac. At the beginning of the covenant, when there was no one outside Abraham and Sarah's family who were allowed in the line, Abraham ordered his servant to go all the way back to Abraham's homeland and family of origin to find a wife for him, so Isaac married Rebekah. They had two sons, but God chose Jacob over Esau. Jacob did the same thing Abraham did—he went back to Abraham's homeland to find a wife. Jacob's children had four mothers, but God chose Leah. Her son Judah continued the promised line because Tamar the Linekeeper saw it through.

There is not much in the story that would explain God's choices. We do not know much about anyone's moral character. Was Abraham exemplary? Did Rebekah do anything particularly good in order to be the one Abraham's servant meets at the well? Was Leah a nicer person than Rachel? Traditional interpretation has infused the characters of these characters with more virtue than the text does. We might look at Abraham and Rebekah and celebrate their willingness to go to an unknown land in response to God's call. We like how the Linekeepers respond with action to the word from God that compels them to protect and prosper Israel.

But none of these are particularly exemplary, and that I think is the point. God simply chose. No one is behaving in any sort of way that could be called distinctively good. As a matter of fact, the who is "in" and who is "out" gets played out in the narrative with some pretty bad behavior.

God makes it clear to Sarah and Abraham that Isaac is the child God has chosen—so the other child, Ishmael, and his mother, Hagar, are exiled from the family. God makes it clear to Rebekah that the one twin in her womb would prevail over the other. Rebekah and Jacob scheme and lie to see God's prophecy through. The twin brothers are alienated from each other for the rest of the story because of their scheming. Jacob finds two wives who come with two maidservants in the land of Abraham's family. The wives, Leah and Rachel, are sisters, but they are constantly at odds with each other as they compete to birth sons. They use Jacob, they exploit their maidservants, and then they have the nerve to name their children names that sound like God played along in their competition.

The story continues, and the twelve brothers who come from the competition between the two sisters hurt and compete with each other even more than their mothers hurt and competed with each other. Jacob has clearly defined favorites among his sons. He blesses them and loves them unevenly.

If we are not reading carefully, we might misunderstand all this choosing. Is this really what God does? Does God have favorites? Why Sarah over Hagar? Why Isaac over Ishmael? Why Leah over Rachel, and why do we disregard their maidservants? Why shouldn't Bilhah or Zilpah carry on the line of God's choosing? Why would they want to? Why must including the lonely barren woman mean excluding the lonely pregnant one?

If we are not reading carefully, we might misunderstand why God allowed Sarah to cast out Hagar and Ishmael. How could God do such a thing? Isn't God a god who cares about everyone? Why does the Bible depict an exclusive God who only cares about and welcomes some while casting out others?

It would seem that when Sarah casts Hagar and Ishmael out of the family in Gen 21, it is the most exclusive thing that could possibly happen. Sarah, mother of nations, throws Hagar out. Abraham, exalted father, lets her, and God sanctions it. There is nothing silent and in the background about God this time. In a story about who is in and who is out, it seems there is no one more out than Hagar and Ishmael. They are out of the family, and they are on the road out of the promised land.

If, however, we understand the purpose of the line, we see these things in a different light. The purpose of the line is that it grows to be a blessing—to use God's words—to *all the families of the earth*. The family God chose benefitted from being in God's covenant line, but it also became the worker of the line. When we look more carefully at Gen 12, when God calls Abraham, God promises to make Abraham a nation and that his name will be great. But this promise was not for Abraham to keep for himself. God gave these things to Abraham in order that they might be used to bless more people—all the families of the earth.

For some reason, at the beginning with Abraham and Sarah, God kept the line exclusive to their family and to the ones God chose within it. But if we are reading in order, we see that quite quickly the line widens to include more and more people within the family that comes from Abraham and Sarah. We have discussed above how Tamar kept the line for Judah, Jacob's son, by Leah. Tamar gave birth to twin sons, Perez and Zerah. We see Perez's name continue in the genealogies, but at about this time in the story, we see an end to such precise and particular choosing on the part of God. The line of Judah continues throughout the story of the Bible, but it grows ever wider. This signals that the exclusion we see in the beginning begins to break open for the inclusion we see for all time.

This is why the connection between Sarah's laughter the second time and her casting out of Ishmael and Hagar is so interesting and so essential to see. Primary exclusion is followed by ultimate inclusion. Ultimate inclusion is the whole purpose of the line of the covenant. Ishmael becomes a picture of this primary exclusion when Sarah casts Hagar and him out, and a picture of ultimate inclusion with Sarah's own words.

Anyone who hears will laugh with me . . .

Sarah's laughter is no simple thing. It is at first like a seed—hidden and dark. It is between God and Sarah. Sarah laughs to herself, and God is the only one who hears it. The first time Sarah laughs is an intimate moment when God appears and tells her that the promised son will come from her. Sarah is the mother of the promise, and all other choices are excluded. But Sarah's laughter from the opening of the tent does not end at the opening of the tent. When her laughter happens again after the promised baby is born, it does something new.

The first time Sarah laughs marks the covenant God shared with Sarah when he came to her tent to tell her she would have a son. The second time Sarah laughs remembers that covenant. Abraham and Sarah would have so many descendants that to count them would be as impossible as counting the sand on the seashore or the stars in the sky. The first time Sarah laughs, it bursts forth from the door of the tent sure as fertility and growth and green new life will burst forth from Sarah. The second time Sarah laughs remembers that the seed to come from Sarah would be prolific. There can be no counting its effect. It will grow and spread to all the nations though all time and in all places.

The first time Sarah laughs she denies it because she is fearful. The second time she laughs, when Isaac is born, it is a wonderful thing—bright and clear for all to hear. Others will join in this laughter. Her laughter the second time celebrates the beginning of what God will do with the covenant. The first time Sarah laughs the hidden barren wife finds out she is included in the Eden thing God is doing. The second time Sarah laughs we discover that the Eden thing God is doing includes everyone who wants to be included.

Amazingly and ironically, this is signified in the narrative by the very person Sarah excludes. The one Sarah kicks out of the family is the one whose story depicts the entire purpose of the line in the first place. We have discussed above how the Linekeepers are drawn by something mysterious to keep the line. Desire? A word from God? We have considered that whether they realize it or not, Sarah and the Linekeepers who come after her are keeping the line God spoke of. When Sarah separates Isaac and Ishmael, saying that Ishmael shall not inherit with Isaac, she is not merely being difficult. For Sarah, there is a line to keep. For Sarah, that line is something to keep exclusive. But for us, we see what happens with the line as the story of Scripture develops. It bursts forth sure as Sarah's laughter bursts forth from the opening of the tent and sure as it will burst forth and include anyone who hears and wants to join in.

Isaac is the line, but Ishmael is the result of it. Isaac is the one who receives the blessing of Abraham, but Ishmael symbolizes all the families who will be blessed. Ishmael signifies the nations, all peoples in all places throughout all time.

If Isaac is the child of the promise, Ishmael is the sand and the stars.

The garden grows in the most unlikely of places, and it overtakes anyone who might hear about it and want in. Shall we have Eden? Shall they? Yes.

THE ROAD AND THE WELL

What is determined in the narrative—who is in and who is out—is blurred in the story of Hagar and Ishmael. Sarah's statement about her laughter and the symbolic use of names is not the only way the narrative depicts inclusion. The narrative overlaps the story of the insiders—Sarah and the children who will come from Sarah—with the story of the outsiders—Hagar and Ishmael. By overlapping the experience of the outsider with the experience of the insider, the narrative builds complexity into the concept of who is in and who is out. If we look carefully behind the story of the insiders, we see that the narrative is hardwiring our understanding of the line. What was narrow widens. What was narrow was always meant to widen.

First, we see this overlap on the road that runs into and out of Egypt and the promised land. Second, we see that like Abraham and like Sarah, Hagar has a covenant confirmation ceremony with God.

THE ROAD

Roads remember, and they look ahead. This road absorbs fear deep into its dry dust. It comes up with the footprints. It remembers fear and it whispers fear . . . do not see, do not hear, you are thrown away.

The stories in Genesis often have to do with places along the routes the characters travel. Sometimes it is hard to tell where in the land the action is taking place, but other times the location of the action is a key to understanding the story.

The Abraham and Sarah narrative begins in Paddan Aram in Haran and the story repeatedly circles back there. There are three journeys between Paddan Aram and the promised land: the first when Abraham and Sarah leave Haran at God's command in Gen 12, the second when Abraham's servant travels back there to find a wife for Isaac in Gen 24, and the third when Jacob runs to Paddan Aram to escape the wrath of his brother Esau in Gen 28–29.

The stretch of this road that is significant to our study begins in the promised land and goes south on the way to Egypt. This stretch is well-traveled in the narrative, too. Genesis 12:8–9 says that Abraham began between Ai and Bethel and journeyed towards the Negeb. From there he went to Egypt because of the famine. This is the road they were on in Gen 12 when Abraham asks Sarah, "Please."

Genesis 13:3–4 tells us that Abraham returned from Egypt by the same route and that he and Sarah settled in Mamre. We might assume Abraham and Sarah are still in Mamre when Hagar makes her first journey towards Egypt in Gen 16 because there is no mention of a move in the narrative, and Gen 18:1 finds Abraham and Sarah still in Mamre.

There is a route that "followed approximately the north-south watershed of the hill country from Shechem via Jerusalem and Bethlehem to Hebron"[1] and continued down through Beersheba toward the Negeb by Beer-lahai-roi on the way through the wilderness of Shur towards Egypt.[2] The way to Shur denotes the more

---

1. Miller and Hayes, *History of Ancient Israel and Judah*, 22.
2. Wright, *Holman Quicksource Bible Atlas*, 110.

southerly of the routes from Canaan to Egypt, from Beersheba via Kadesh-Barnea."[3] Since both Abraham and Sarah's Gen 12 journey to Egypt and Hagar's Gen 16 journey to Egypt began in Mamre, and since Beer-lahai-roi is the well Hagar meets the angel of the Lord, it makes sense that they would have traveled the very same road.

According to Gen 35:27 and 37:1, Jacob also settled in the region of Mamre in Canaan. This is where Jacob lived when he sent Joseph to Shechem from "the valley of Hebron" in Genesis to check on his brothers. Joseph's route into Egypt when his brothers sold him there differed from Sarah and Hagar's and from his brothers' treks back and forth because it began in Dothan and likely took the northern trade route along the sea.[4] But the journeys of the brothers between Egypt and Mamre during the famine, and Jacob's final trek into Egypt, took the same route Sarah took in her travels and Hagar took in Gen 16. We know this because her route went from Mamre and the valley of Hebron through Beersheba.[5]

Roads remember and look ahead. Sarah the beautiful, her children the jealous. Hagar's name floats lonely. It means wanderer. Brothers move as if the road is covered quickly. Wanderer sees death and sees God as if the road is endless. Jacob the fearful has had roadside dreams before. Does Jacob's fear remember Sarah's? Did Sarah fear? There is something to fear. Fear comes up with the footprints with the dust. It lifts off the ground and swirls in the air and whispers. Stories echo.

This road is one of the keys to understanding the story. The mother of the chosen son travels this road into Egypt and slavery in Pharaoh's harem. She travels it back to the promised land when God hears her and delivers her out of Egypt. The mother of the cast-out son runs on this road towards Egypt and freedom and home only to be told by God to return to the promised land, Sarah's oppressive hand, and slavery. God draws both women back to the promised land on this road. Both women give Abraham a

3. Wenham, *Word Biblical Commentary*, 16–50.

4. Wright, *Holman Quicksource Bible Atlas*, 112–13.

5. Wright, *Holman Quicksource Bible Atlas*, 112–13.

son there. Sarah is home because God heard her from Egypt and put her right back on that road. Because of Sarah, it goes well for Abraham. Because of God, it goes well for Sarah. She finds herself safe back in her tent.

It is a bit the same and a bit different for Hagar. Instead of hearing her, God sees her. Hagar says it outright. She names God something that has to do with God and Hagar seeing each other. Instead of God naming her back, God names her son something that has to do with how God is a god of hearing. God sees her, but God turns her around and sends her back the way she came. It goes well for Abraham because of this. Hagar gives Abraham a son. It will ultimately go well for Hagar. God promises her that she will be the mother of a great nation. She is a matriarch among the patriarchs—the beginning of a nation.

Generations later, the twelve tribes of Israel travel this same road into Egypt. Unlike Hagar, they make it. Like Hagar, this road leads to slavery. Like Sarah, all Sarah's seed will be enslaved in Egypt. Like Hagar, slavery will oppress, and they will eventually run too. Like Sarah, they cry out. Like Ishmael, God hears them. Like Hagar, God meets them in the wilderness with promises, and like Hagar, God draws them into the promised land.

We look up from our Bibles and we wonder. Does it mean anything that insiders and outsiders alike experience fear and running and wandering on this very same road? Back and forth humanity does what humanity does regardless of who they are. Help like the help of God is lost. There is something about this road between Egypt and the promised land that makes us see it all so clearly. Humanity creates desolation for itself everywhere. We become wanderers in and out of slavery in one way or another because help like the help of God is lost among us.

HAGAR'S COVENANT
CONFIRMATION CEREMONY

Sarah is used to beauty. She has heard the word swirl around her since she began remembering words. "Sarah is beautiful" is the refrain that never got swallowed up by "Sarah is barren." Beauty larger than bar-renness is really something. But old appeared and swallowed beauty. Sarah finds her eyes resting often on young opaque strong smooth as if had she only observed her own young opaque strong smooth, she might have somehow held on to it.

It is common to think that Sarah threw Hagar away because she was jealous. The text does not tell us that. What the text does say is that once Hagar knew she was pregnant, Hagar looked small at Sarah. Infuriating, especially since Sarah meant for the opposite to happen. Sarah figured that through Hagar she would be built up. We might also wonder if Sarah was jealous of Hagar because she was young and fertile and Sarah was anything but young and fertile. This may be so. The text does not tell us, so we do not know. We might think about it though. Either way Sarah's efforts result in what turns out to be lonely and alienating. The garden is far away.

Sarah appeals to Abraham. This thing that has happened, the wrong Hagar has done to Sarah, is something Sarah says is a wrong as deep as violence. She wills that violence back on Abraham. May this wrong, heavy on me, be heavy on you. The destruction of unity has left enough space for violence to fly in the air between Abraham and Sarah, and so Abraham pushes it away from himself and back onto Sarah. He puts Hagar in Sarah's hands, and he washes his own. Sarah takes that violence back and does more violence. Like dry parched ground swallowing flowers in a famine, old and barren works pain on young and fertile. So, Abraham sends the mother and son away.

But the experience of the outsider continues to overlap with the experience of the insider. Abraham, Sarah, and Hagar all have covenant confirmation ceremonies.

Sarah's covenant ceremony happens when God comes to her tent. It is marked by her laughter and by God's hearing and affirming it. She is the mother of the covenant—she is the one God has chosen.

Abraham's covenant ceremony happens when God calls him a father and tells him to be circumcised and to circumcise the men of his household. Abraham's covenant confirmation is also marked by laughter. Even so, he obeys. Abraham is opened and ready for the Eden thing that God will do.

Hagar is most decidedly not included in the covenant God has just confirmed with Abraham and Sarah, but God comes to Hagar too—not to the opening of a tent but to a well. There is deep significance to the fact that this meeting happens at a well. This is Hagar's own covenant confirmation ceremony.

Like tents, wells are special places in the story of the Bible too. A motif runs through Genesis and picks up again with Moses and his wife in Exodus and then again in Ruth. It has to do with wells and marriage arrangements. Wells are the places where betrothals happen.[6]

There are signals in the narrative that alert us to notice when one of these special betrothals at a well is happening. They begin with a future bridegroom or his servant coming to a well after having completed a long journey from a foreign land. At the well, the traveler encounters a girl. I say "girl" because the pattern uses either the Hebrew word for "girl" (*na arah*) or a phrase identifying the person as a daughter. Someone, either the traveler or the girl, draws water from the well. After the interchange, the girl hurries home to tell her family about the arrival of the traveler. At some point in all this action the family agrees on a betrothal between the girl and the traveler, or between the girl and the person who sent the traveler.[7]

Each betrothal scene contains variations on the pattern. It is really important that we note the variations because they give us clues to the significance of a passage. Moments at wells between a man and a woman are so significant that when we see one, it should make us think of all the others. When we see a variation within the theme, it should make us wonder what the meaning of that variation is. We can look at the betrothals of Isaac and

6. Alter, *Art of Biblical Narrative*, 55–71.

7. These are Alter's specifications to watch for in this betrothal at a well type-scene. He also talks about the importance of looking for variations on the theme. Alter does not include Hagar's moment at the well with the angel of Yahweh in his exposition of well type-scenes. I do not know why because it seems quite clear.

Rebekah, and Jacob and Rachel in Genesis. There are key differences that help us to understand not only these betrothals that happen in Genesis but also other betrothals at wells, like the one between Moses and Zipporah in Exodus, and even—by really studying the variations—the betrothal between Ruth and Boaz in the book of Ruth.

This is exactly what we can do with Hagar. We find her at a well in Gen 16 after running away from Sarah's oppressive hand, and we think about the other times we have seen key women at wells. It is particularly important when we look at Hagar for us to see how her well moment breaks the pattern we have seen with the Genesis matriarchs.

Right away it is obvious that what happens at the well between the angel of the Lord and Hagar is no betrothal. However, it is impossible to miss the betrothal imagery and the twists Hagar's well scene makes with the pattern. The matriarchs' well scenes involve a young girl or daughter of an important man. Hagar is no daughter. She, like Sarah, has no named parentage in a genealogy. Not only is she not a daughter or a young girl, but she is a "slave-girl." A daughter of an important man is a far cry from the slave-girl of an oppressive women. She is however a traveler, and she comes to a well. In the betrothal type-scenes of Genesis, the bridegroom or his servant is the traveler, and the woman draws water for him. There is no bridegroom for Hagar. Instead, the angel of the Lord approaches her.

Unlike the other well/betrothal scenes in Genesis, no one draws water from this well. However, like the classic well/betrothal scene, Hagar leaves the well and goes back in the direction she came. In the matriarchs' well/betrothal scenes, Rachel and Rebekah run from the well back home to announce to their families what has just happened. They gather their people for a meal. A betrothal is agreed upon and enacted, and a new family arrangement is birthed.

Like the matriarchs, Hagar leaves the well and goes back in the direction she came. Unlike the matriarchs, the place she returns to is far from home. She turns back from her journey towards home in Egypt and returns to the oppressive family arrangement that was so oppressive it moved her to run in the first place.

The angel of the Lord reminds us hauntingly of Abraham, who on this very road asked Sarah "please." Please take this road into slavery in Egypt. The angel of the Lord does not ask Hagar "please." Instead, Hagar is told to return to slavery in the promised land. Like Sarah, Hagar obeys. She will agree to this covenant even if it means returning to oppression.

Like the matriarchs, this well meeting results in a new family arrangement. Hagar turns back and will give birth to a son for Abraham in the land God promised. Like the patriarchs, the Lord tells Hagar that her offspring will be multiplied to such a degree that they cannot be counted.

There is nothing funny about finding yourself in a pit. There might be something sickly laughable when you look up out over the edge and see how others have what you do not. Maybe that sort of thing is more strange than funny. Strange how life works differently for some than for others. Motherless and fatherless and homeless and wandering. Sarah's arms ache for a baby and Hagar's heart aches for home. The tear is deep, and the garden is far, and no one helps anyone.

We look up from our Bibles and we wonder again. Is God a god who stands watching blithely from afar? No. This time God is not far off; God is right there on the road with her. God sends her back into oppression only for Abraham and Sarah to cast her out again thirteen years later. The question is not "why does God allow this?" The question is "why is God a part of this?" What solace is there for Hagar if she is the mother of the wrong nation? Is it enough that God promises to hear her son? Does it mean anything that the road is the same for the insider as it is for the outsider? How much does a promise pay for someone who finds herself in a pit?

If we do not understand the purpose of the line, these questions hang in a way that reflects the curse after the matter of the tree instead of the unity that existed before it. We are angered and hurt by what we think is the answer to these questions, for we too are victims of the disaster of the tree. We are apt to see disunity in places where we really ought to see different people on the same road. But God hears a hidden woman sure as God hears a cast-out son. The hurt is the work of disunified humanity. The hearing is the work of God. And this is where Sarah's laughter echoes again. Despite the disaster that would cause all humanity to disregard and cast out, to create desolation everywhere, her laughter simply reminds us that God hears. It assures us that God affirms the pain that comes of the disaster and the complicated stuff that gets mixed in with the laugh Sarah laughed. And if God hears and affirms Sarah's laughter, surely God will hear all who would come from her. Surely, God will hear anyone who might laugh along.

Sometimes the meanings of words fly higher than what a character might understand. The first time Sarah laughs she denies laughter because she is afraid. The second time she laughs she denies laughter to the ones she casts out. The mother of all the nations of all the earth in all times and in all places casts out the outsider. But the name God names Sarah, "Mother of Nations," and the words she laughs with her laughter, "anyone who hears will laugh with me," contradict her. Her laughter is no longer just hers from God. It gathers stars. It lands on the ground and sprouts seeds. The garden grows in the most unlikely of places. And even if Abraham would disregard Sarah, and Sarah would throw away Hagar and Ishmael, God will not do such things.

Laughter bursts forth and swirls in the air and gathers stars and scoops up sand. Laughter spins around and laughs back at Sarah. Laughter will cast a wide net despite the desire of the one who bore her.

A WORD ABOUT UNITY

If we think about the matter of the tree as something that tore apart the unity God intended, we see it. He Laughs and God Hears should have been true brothers. The Mother of Nations and the Wanderer should have been friends. Abraham and Sarah were meant to protect each other. Shouldn't it go well? Help like the help of God everywhere like stars and sand.

If the moment at Sarah's tent is only about Sarah and God and the chosen line, it leaves all other people in all other places and times unaccounted for. If the mark of the covenant remains a mark on a man, it excludes everyone else. If the Eden thing God is doing hangs on humanity's love and ability to hear cries, desolation remains.

The road and the covenant at the well are layers upon the names of the sons that remind us of this. From the beginning of the line, from the moment God called Abraham and Sarah, God had all the families of the earth in mind. It is not a small thing that the laughter of a hidden and cast-aside woman would signify this inclusion. It is a pondersome thing that the laughter of the woman who would cast out another person is the very thing that signifies the great bringing in that God intended then and still intends today . . . so that it may go well.

God's choice of Sarah always stood despite Abraham's failures. The line the Linekeepers kept was never truly exclusive if its purpose was always to bring people in. It is here we must never mistake what people have said about God, and what the word of God is saying about God. God is the God who hears. There is no outsider. Anyone who hears and wants to laugh along is "in."

WHY DID SARAH LAUGH?

Is there even an answer to such a question? God asks it and no one answers. The text does not tell us, so we do not know.

But laughter is born of things, and it gives birth to things. Things of dust and things of a garden. It is contagious and it spreads unrestricted and uncontained, and it is for everyone who wants to join in. Everyone. It swirls in the air and does something new. It is not hidden or hoarded. It is not one thing for those in the shadows and another for those in the daylight.

It can come from the desolation of the pit or the place of barren loneliness. Often it is something no one hears. It is something, as Sarah says, that comes from God. It seems it is a thing of the garden—that beautiful old garden God remembers all the way back to the time when things began and when God first began loving humanity.

Maybe God falls into laughter with us like one who dearly misses unity. God does not deny things in our lives even if they are confusing. No. God hears and remembers.

Yes, you did laugh.

Bibliography

Alter, Robert. *The Art of Biblical Narrative*. Rev. and updated ed. New York: Basic, 2011.

Brown, Raymond E. *The Sensus Plenior of Sacred Scripture*. Eugene, OR: Wipf & Stock, 2008.

Brueggemann, Walter. *An Introduction to the Old Testament: The Canon and Christian Imagination*. Louisville: Westminster John Knox, 2007.

Carter, Jimmy. "Why I Believe the Mistreatment of Women Is The Number One Human Rights Abuse." TED. Jun. 30, 2015. YouTube video, 16:36. https://youtu.be/aZZYlpfZ-iA.

Meyers, Carol L. *Discovering Eve: Ancient Israelite Women in Context*. New York: Oxford University Press, 1988.

Miller, J. Maxwell, and John H. Hayes. *A History of Ancient Israel and Judah*. 2nd ed. Louisville: Westminster John Knox, 2006.

Sharp, Carolyn J. *Wrestling the Word: The Hebrew Scriptures and the Christian Believer*. Louisville: Westminster John Knox, 2010.

Trible, Phyllis. *God and the Rhetoric of Sexuality*. Overtures to Biblical Theology 2. Philadelphia: Fortress, 1978.

VanGemeren, Willem A. *The New International Dictionary of Old Testament Theology and Exegesis*. Grand Rapids: Zondervan, 2012.

Wenham, Gordon J. *Word Biblical Commentary: Genesis 16–50*. Vol. 2. Dallas: Word, 2017.

Wright, Paul. *Holman Quicksource Bible Atlas: With Charts and Biblical Reconstructions*. Nashville: Broadman & Holman, 2005.

www.ingramcontent.com/pod-product-compliance
Lightning Source LLC
Chambersburg PA
CBHW060405090426
42734CB00011B/2265